GRIEVING WITH GRACE

Grieving With Grace

A

WOMAN'S

PERSPECTIVE

Dolores R. Leckey

ST. ANTHONY MESSENGER PRESS
Cincinnati, Ohio

Excerpts from "To Live with the Spirit," from *The Selected Poetry of Jessica Powers,* are used with permission of ICS Publications, Washington, D.C. All copyrights, Carmelite Monastery, Pewaukee, WI.

Scripture passages have been taken from *New Revised Standard Version Bible,* copyright ©1989 by the Division of Christian Education of the National Council of the Churches of Christ in the U.S.A., and used by permission. All rights reserved.

LIBRARY OF CONGRESS CATALOGING-IN-PUBLICATION DATA
Leckey, Dolores R.
Grieving with grace : a woman's perspective / Dolores R. Leckey.
p. cm. — (Called to holiness: spirituality for Catholic women)
Includes bibliographical references.
ISBN 978-0-86716-888-4 (pbk. : alk. paper) 1. Bereavement—Religious aspects—Catholic Church. 2. Grief—Religious aspects—Catholic Church. 3. Church year. 4. Catholic women—Religious life. 5. Leckey, Dolores R. I. Title.
BX2373.B47L43 2008
248.8'66082—dc22
2008020344

ISBN 978-0-86716-888-4

Copyright ©2008, Dolores R. Leckey. All rights reserved.

Published by St. Anthony Messenger Press
28 W. Liberty St.
Cincinnati, OH 45202
www.SAMPBooks.org
www.CalledtoHoliness.org

Printed in the United States of America.

Printed on acid-free paper.

08 09 10 11 12   5 4 3 2 1

Dedicated
To the memory of
TPL

"... at my back I always hear
Time's winged chariot hurrying near."
— Andrew Marvell[1]

CONTENTS

ACKNOWLEDGMENTS

I am grateful for the encouragement and support of many people in bringing this book to life. In the winter of 2005 I attended a Catholic Writers' Retreat at the Redemptorist Spiritual Life Center in Picture Rocks, Arizona. There I raised the possibility of writing a book based on a personal journey of discovering life through death. I presented the outline of this book and the writers and publishers who were present were more than encouraging. I came home ready to create a book based on this personal experience. That affirmation was very important for me as I proceeded to turn a journal into a book.

When Elizabeth Dreyer, general editor of this *Called to Holiness* series invited me to contribute a volume, I wondered if this project of my heart would fit. Elizabeth encouraged me to think it would. Along the way she offered counsel and insight, and for all, I am grateful.

I'm indebted to the people who read this book in its unedited version and offered suggestions for improvement. John Haughey, S.J., Senior Fellow at the Woodstock Theological Center; Doctor Dana Greene, director of the Aquinas Institute at Emory University; Doctor Richard Giannone of Fordham University's English Department; Brian McDermott, S.J., of Loyola College, Baltimore; and Rhoda Nary of the Shalem staff were all generous with their time and expertise in critiquing the text. They were an enormous help to me.

My colleagues at the Woodstock Theological Center have been quietly supportive of this project, not pressuring me to tell them "what the book is about" (which would have been hard to do at different stages). Their trust in what I have been doing all these months is evident. I am especially grateful to Maria Ferrara, administrative assistant at Woodstock, who not only assisted me with the technology of production, but offered insightful suggestions along the way. I appreciate her colleagueship, but more, her friendship.

*The focus of this series is spirituality. Its interest is women of all back-*grounds: rich and poor; married and single; white, black and brown; gay and straight; those who are biological mothers and those who are mothers in other senses. There will be volumes on grassroots theology, family life, prayer, action for justice, grieving, young adult, wisdom years and Hispanic heritage. I hope all the volumes in this series will deepen and shape your own spiritual life in creative ways, as you engage with the theology of our rich, two-thousand-year-old Christian tradition.

Women's spiritualities are lived in light of their concrete, specific experiences of joy and struggle; ecstasy and despair; virtue and vice; work and leisure; family and friends; embodiment and sexuality; tears and laughter; sickness and health; sistering and mothering. These volumes are for women and men from all walks of life, whether they are new to the spiritual journey or old hands, affluent, middle-class or poor. Included in the circle we call church are persons from every country on the planet, some at the center, others at the margins or even beyond.

The time is ripe for "ordinary" women to be doing theology. The first and second waves of the women's movement in the nineteenth and twentieth centuries provided a valiant and solid foundation for the third wave which will mark, and be marked by, the world of the early twenty-first century. Changes and developments from one generation to the next makes our heads spin. Younger women readers are likely to be already grooming the soil for a fourth wave of Christian spirituality done by and for women. Women have always loved God, served others and struggled with sin, but the historical context has been less than friendly in terms of women's dignity, acknowledgment of female gifts and empowerment by church and society. In a time of growing emphasis on the role of clergy, and the backlash against women in society, the voices of the laity—especially the voices of women—are needed more than ever.

The Greek language has two words for time. *Chronos* points to the time signaled by the hands on the clock—for example, it is a quarter past two. *Kairos* points to time that is ripe, a moment pregnant with possibility. As Christian women, we live in a time rightly described as *kairos*. It is a time that calls us, demands of us renewed energy, reflection and commitment to attend to and help each other grow spiritually as we seek to love ourselves and the world. At this point in history, the fruit of women's struggle includes new self-awareness, self-confidence and self-respect. More and more women are beginning to see just how lovable and capable they are. The goal of the Christian life has always been to lay down our lives in love for the other, but the particular ways this vocation is lived out differ from era to era and place to place. Women's ability to voice with confidence the phrase, "I am a theologian" at the beginning of the twenty-first century means something it could not have meant even fifty years ago.

Those who were part of the early waves of feminism celebrate the hard-won accomplishments of the women's movement and know that this work needs to be taken up by future generations. Young women in their twenties and thirties are often unaware of past efforts that brought about more dignity and freedom for women. Women have opened many doors, but many remain closed. The media have recently explored the plight of Hindu widows in India; less publicized is that women in the United States still earn only seventy-seven cents for every dollar earned by their male counterparts. We must be vigilant and continue to act for decades to come in order to secure our accomplishments thus far and make further inroads toward the creation of a just, egalitarian world. Those who sense that the women's movement is in a doldrums inspire us to renew the enthusiasm and dedication of our foremothers.

When we cast our eye beyond the women of our own nation, it takes but a split-second to realize that the majority of the world's poor and oppressed are women. A quick visit to the Women's Human Rights Watch Web site reveals the breadth and depth of women's oppression across the globe from poverty and domestic abuse to sex slavery. Most women (and their children) do not have enough to eat, a warm, dry place to sleep or access to education. Female babies are more at risk than male babies. Women, more than men, lack the protection of the law and the respect of their communities. The double-standard in sexual matters affects women in harmful ways in all cultures and economic groups across the globe.

For all of these reasons it is not just important—but pressing, crucial, urgent—that all women of faith own the title "theologian" and shape this role in light of each woman's unique set of characteristics, context, relationships and spiritualities. We are theologians when we sort through our experience and the great and small problems of our time through reflection on Scripture or the words of a mystic or theologian. The images of God that emerged for Paul, Augustine or Catherine of Siena provide guidance, but their theology cannot ever be a substitute for our own. Theology helps us shape what we think about God, justice, love, the destiny of humanity and the entire universe in a way that is relevant to the specific issues facing us in the twenty-first century. The call to spiritual depths and mystical heights has never been more resounding.

Elizabeth A. Dreyer
Series Editor

There are many ways in which the course of our daily life is altered. The ravages of war can cause the loss of home, business and loved ones, as we see in Iraq year after year. So, too, with natural disasters. After a tornado leveled an entire town in the Midwest, I heard a woman who had survived say on the radio, "I have to reinvent my life." When a whole way of life is changed, the greatest loss may be that of hope.

On a smaller scale, a chronic illness can require changes in daily living, limiting our options, and forcing us to choose different priorities. The altering may be gradual, as it is when we age, losing mobility, or hearing, or our independence. It is death, however, that alters life forever. This is especially true with the death of a spouse, the person with whom all the rhythms of daily living have been shared, at all levels: body, mind and soul.

In all cases we experience some shift in consciousness, some change in the way we see the world, ourselves and God. This is the point at which an authentic change of direction may begin, a change for the better, what Christians refer to as *conversion*. Initially, we may be so intent on survival that we do not view the change as a conversion. But in the midst of survival, and all its attending techniques, we can sense the challenge to find ways to get in touch with the richness of life *here and now*, and to welcome the next chapters of a life newly unfolding. Therein lie the seeds of resurrection.

More than twenty years ago, novelist and poet Reynolds Price was diagnosed with cancer of the spine. He was treated and lived, but his way of living was completely changed. Though he is now wheelchair bound, he writes that these last decades have been the most creative and productive of his entire life, and his work confirms that.

When he realized the enormous change that had taken place he asked himself: Who will you be tomorrow? That, I think, is a question that all of us in the midst of change or conversion might ask ourselves.

A Personal Narrative

The question I framed a few years ago was this: How is it possible to realize a future of creativity filled with God's abundant love when my heart is broken? My heart broke early in the morning of June 23, 2003. My husband, Tom, who had suffered from serious cardiac problems for years, went to the hospital on our forty-sixth wedding anniversary, not because of a cardiac event but because he had bronchitis and couldn't stop coughing. He remained overnight for observation, not in intensive care, but in an ordinary hospital room. We fully expected he would come home the next day.

At 5:30 the next morning my phone rang. I knew immediately it was the hospital.

"How is my husband?" I asked. A doctor said, "I'm sorry to tell you...he's not going to make it. He tried to get out of bed and hit the floor; people are working on him, but he has no pulse." This doctor— a stranger to me—then ordered me not to drive and she called my son. I called my pastor. All this bad news was being conveyed by phone, and with every number dialed I could feel my heart breaking, piece by piece. I remembered a poem about how bad news always comes by phone; before a word is spoken you can sense that life is now different.

Our children, all of whom were in town for our anniversary, joined me in the hospital room where their father, still warm, remained. My pastor came, bringing experience born of dealing with losses and lamentations. There was oil for anointing, the prayer of commendation ("May the martyrs welcome you") and sacred bread to remind us that we all belonged to one another, and to Christ, and that would never change. Hours passed, and Tom grew cold. It was time to go home.

At home I stared at a woodcut of the Sacred Heart by Robert McGovern which we have had in our home for many years. For so long I had prayed to the Sacred Heart ("heal his heart...," "bring peace to our hearts...," "give me a loving heart...") and now a Jesuit friend stood in my dining room and suggested that the devotion is rooted in marital love. And so I buried my beloved with his bruised and battered heart on the Feast of the Sacred Heart.

Home. The place of shared life in all its joys and sorrows was now profoundly silent. I who have always cherished silence and solitude experienced it in a different way: the silence of absence. At first it was overwhelming. Alone I wept and groaned, sounds reminiscent of Irish keening. I struggled to get balance, some understanding of life in the present. Three old trustworthy aids came to me. One was writing, the others ritual and prayer. They wove in and out of each other.[1]

Many books about grief were given to me, some of them modern classics such as C.S. Lewis's *A Grief Observed*. They were not what I needed. Then I came across a book by mystery writer P.D. James, *Time to Be in Earnest*. It was not a grief book but a memoir of sorts, covering one year in her life—her seventy-seventh. What I saw in those pages was a woman, a wife and a mother, who had lived alone for many years because of her husband's mental illness. The account of ordinary days and nights was both consoling and energizing. I needed to see meaningful patterns in the lives of those living alone, and P.D. James fulfilled that need.

At the end of the summer, as my lamentations slowly subsided, I began my own journal. At first I wrote as a way of coping. My focus was a particular love—our love—and writing was a way of connecting to that love. But in the writing, and the living, of days, weeks and months, a story of different proportions began to emerge. Love stretched. The communion of saints, a cornerstone of Catholic belief enshrined in the creeds of Christian faith, became palpable. Traditionally the communion of saints has referred to the dead only.

The communion I experienced included not only my husband, but friends, public figures, culture in its many forms, and the social contexts in which we all live. The difference between loneliness and aloneness took on a new clarity as my life experience expanded into communion. I began to probe the meaning of resurrection, our resurrection, the resurrection of the body, or, as earlier translations of the creed stated, the resurrection of the flesh. I had given it little thought before, but now I had the desire to understand what this means.

Why This Book?

The decision to write this book can be traced to the idea that the most personal human experience is also the most universal—like Eucharist. Hence, journal entries, some of them deeply personal, form a key element in this book's structure. These entries are not really spiritual journal-writing. There is no crisis of soul evident in the entries, although there are crises recorded, large and small. But mostly they are about everyday things. I realize now that I chose this mundane form because what I needed was to recognize in the dynamics of everyday domestic and professional life the traces of God, and the dynamism of grace. That's what I spotted in the P.D. James book, although it does not move from the experience to theological reflection, which I try to do. (By theological reflection, I mean a form of theologizing that draws upon lived experience as much as classic texts.)[2] The journal covers one year, from September 2003 to September 2004. Some narratives and theological reflections were added later.

Divided into four chapters, this book follows the liturgical cycle of the year: Ordinary Time (chapter one), Advent, Christmas and Epiphany (chapter two), Lent and Easter (chapter three), and Pentecost, the extended season of the Holy Spirit lived in Ordinary Time (chapter four). The influence of Bernard Lonergan, S.J., is seen in the structure: Journal entries provide the data of experience; there is reflection on the data in an effort to reach understanding; there is the desire for responsible action; and throughout, there is questioning and the recognition of art as a bearer of meaning. Initially, this influence was unconscious, but over time I saw what was happening. Vespers is the centerpiece of my reflections.

About Vespers

Monasteries are places where Saint Paul's directive to "pray always" is taken seriously. Since the Second Vatican Council, it is less usual for monks and nuns to rise in the middle of the night for prayer. (Trappists—men and women—are one exception.) Rather, the rhythms of our waking moments are honored in prayer. Morning Prayer typically occurs in the early hours of the day, at sunrise or shortly thereafter. Midday Prayer is around noon, and Vespers is prayed as evening descends. The last prayer of the cycle is Compline, the prayer just before sleep. The sun is gone; only moonlight, starlight and lamplight guide our final steps. The blessing in that final prayer of the day is one my husband and I said for many years: "May the Almighty Lord grant us a restful night and a peaceful death." As my husband's health deteriorated it became an ever more precious prayer. But it is Vespers that guides me daily.

I think of this book as celebrating Vesper time for several reasons. A central one is that Evening Prayer became a support for me in my loss and mourning. It also has been, and is, an open door to the abundant life that pours from the heart of God. I have always loved evening. The sky changes color, lights go on in homes, and there is a feel of Dutch paintings with their emphasis on the interior. Sometimes the sun and the moon appear simultaneously. Vespers, filled with psalms of praise and longing, struggle and truth, climaxing with Mary's prayer, the Magnificat, provided a doorway to other forms of prayer, like silence—not the silence of absence that had been so painful in the first months after Tom's death, but the silence of a rich presence. I felt at ease talking with Tom, asking for guidance which unfailingly showed up in some form. Talking to the dead might seem strange, but it is clearly embedded in Catholic tradition.

Vesper time also refers to this particular period of my life (and the lives of many women) when we are vividly aware of the passage of time, just as evening reminds us of the passage of a day. So I think of this "third third" of life (a term used by a physician friend) as Vesper time. It's a time to reflect on what has been, to be grateful for what is, and to prepare for nightfall.

CHAPTER ONE

• Ordinary Time •

*Probing the sacred in the ordinary through
remembrance and friendship*

What Is Ordinary Time?

Ordinary Time in the church's cycle represents the steady routine of
daily life. Nothing special, nothing to distract from the quotidian
rhythms that characterize most of our days and nights. It comes after
the feasting of Christmas, the introspection of Lent, the joy of Easter,
and the life-changing arrival of the Holy Spirit at Pentecost. I don't
know anyone who doesn't appreciate Ordinary Time with its plain-
ness and balance of work, study, leisure and prayer. Ordinary Time is
the starting point for my journal entries. Strange then, perhaps, that I
began my writing about loss and changed life on September 11, 2003.
Nothing about 9/11 was or is ordinary. It became the catalyst for our
nation to declare that we were in a new kind of war, a war on terror.
It is a war that seems to have no end, and no set armies or battle lines
or criteria for declaring peace.

Journal Entries
September 11, 2003
While the nation mourned the second anniversary of the event we
have come to know simply as 9/11, I went to Columbia Gardens to
visit Tom's (and someday my own) grave, carrying red carnations and

a reservoir of tears. Cathartic tears. These cemetery visits are important to me echoing, perhaps, the cemetery rituals so vivid in Latina spirituality.

Returning home I stared at a mural on our living room wall, a reproduction of the ancient fresco in Priscilla's catacombs that was installed in our home on September 11, 2001. I awoke early that morning eager to greet the installers. The catacombs of Priscilla are a favorite place of mine, a place of quiet and respite in the busy city of Rome. Maybe I like it because those catacombs are the home of the second-century Roman matron who ran a household, welcomed guests, worried about her children and husband and who happened to be a Christian. Not so different from women around the world and across time. This particular painting is of a small group of women sitting at a table. There is bread, a cup of wine, and baskets on the floor. It is called "The Breaking of the Bread." The blue and sepia colors, the colors of antiquity, and the composition of people gathered in friendship and hope convey an aura of peace. That is our mural. In Priscilla's catacombs, it is one of several outstanding frescoes.

As the installers prepared for their work, my phone rang. It was about 8:55 AM. Our daughter Celia, who lives quite close to the Pentagon, asked if we were all right. "Of course," I answered. Then she told me about events in New York, where my husband and I grew up. The TV was now on and we and the installers stared in disbelief at the frightening images. Celia called again. Her small eighty-year-old cottage was rattling from the Pentagon explosion. She told me another plane was headed toward Washington and said she was going to the nearby high school her son attended.

Forty minutes later she was sitting with us sipping water. She had walked the mile and a half to the school after a national guardsman on bicycle told her she couldn't drive; the streets had to be kept clear. The mural installers tried to call their homes but the lines were busy. I tried to call family in New York City but there was only an automatic message available: "Due to an emergency your call cannot be completed."

And so it was for the next week.

By noon that day "The Breaking of the Bread" had been installed and fighter planes could be heard in the sky above. Now two years later I marvel at how blocked, mercifully blocked, is our foresight. For a quarter of a century, Tom and I lived at the edge of death. We used to laughingly count how many of his nine lives had been used. We could not know that on the second anniversary of our national tragedy he would be in the grave. "The grave's a fine and private place / but none I think do there embrace." Tom put these lines from Andrew Marvell's poem "To His Coy Mistress" on our gravestone a few months before his death. How often he read that poem to me over the years. Getting the gravestone ready was one of his last projects and we negotiated on precisely which lines would go below my choice of verses from Psalm 138: "When I called you answered me / You built up strength within me."

I look at the mural and remember that it is located in a cemetery of sorts. Christians of Priscilla's time must have loved coming to her house (as I do) and I can understand their wanting to be buried there. I look at the mural and remember how thousands of lives were shattered on 9/11. Children, spouses, friends, lovers gone in a flash. It would be several years before I would fathom how forgiveness and reconciliation rose out of the ashes of that dreadful day.

Yesterday I spent some time at the post office preparing a special-delivery envelope that would carry the final check for our mortgage: good use of insurance money, per Tom's request. My parents told me that when they paid off their mortgage (in the 1930s) they burned the mortgage papers in the fireplace. That has a little more panache than special delivery.

I also bought some stamps, choosing the memorial for the Korean War. Tom volunteered for the draft the day the truce for that war was signed. He was nineteen and a student at St. Michael's College in Toronto. Joining the army was his rebellion against his father, or so he analyzed his rather rash action. A year later we met.

Armed with the memorial stamps I headed for the florist and bought some yellow roses on sale. Their fragrance filled the house which was both a surprise and a delight. (Forced roses rarely live up to their expectations). The roses also released a stream of memories of our time at the Lay Academy in Bad Boll, Germany, in 1979. The academy held a conference on healthcare and our study of the subject included a trip to the Freiderklinic in Stuttgart. The hospital is constructed in accord with the philosophy of Rudolph Steiner, and is quite an amazing place. There are no square rooms because nothing in nature is square. Every room looks out on the garden. In the morning patients are awakened by the sound of an alpine horn. The arts are central to the clinic's philosophy of healing. Patients listen to music and are encouraged to play an instrument. There are regular poetry readings, and patients attend plays. In every room there are bouquets of roses. Elixir of roses is given to patients and visitors because the rose is believed to be the flower of health. The delicate fragrance of the fresh flowers I had just bought proved the point.

Memories of the Freiderklinic and the presence of "The Breaking of the Bread" in my home drew me into an awareness of how art and nature are simply "there," ever-present stimulants for healing and for choosing life. Yet, it is we who must choose to let the healing happen.

September 12, 2003
A rainy, rainy day. I attended the regularly scheduled seminar at the Woodstock Theological Center at Georgetown University. We discussed the common good and agreed to begin a study of the documents of the Thirty-Fourth General Congregation of the Society of Jesus which was held in 1995. The ongoing seminar provides an opportunity for those who work at the center (the fellows) to learn more about one another, how we think and how experience influences

us. These face-to-face meetings with colleagues are one of my lifelines right now.

After a long day of meetings I arrived home at 6:15 PM tired and wet. Among my phone messages was an invitation from my son Tommy to join his family for dinner, something I enjoy so much. My need for concrete human connection is enormous. Tonight, however, prudence won over desire. The busyness of the past week and the long day made it clear that I needed to be home this rainy and windy night. Vespers provided respite and wisdom. I recited Psalm 116 aloud and slowly, and experienced it as the prayer of my heart.

> You have delivered my soul from death
> my eyes from tears
> my feet from stumbling
> I walk before the Lord
> In the land of the living

I savor the last line. This is my world, I say to myself, and to Tom and to God. The world in which I live is the land of the living. It sinks in ever so slowly.

And what characterizes the land of the living I ask? Clues are found in the prayer for Friday Vespers. "You have called us not to bestow gifts, but to bestow ourselves freely, relying with unhesitating confidence on your providence. May we live in this spirit of generosity, gladly sharing the goodness with which you have blessed us."

The land of the living is marked by sharing.

September 20, 2003
Hurricane Isabel swept through the Washington metro area two days ago, and the results (downed trees and electric lines) are still with us. I ventured out to Clarendon Baptist Church to a forum on affordable housing and social justice. The forum, which is slated to become an annual event, is to be named the Thomas P. Leckey Memorial Forum, in honor of Tom's dedicated work to secure an adequate supply of

affordable rental properties in Arlington, Virginia. To that end he and I along with three other couples began in 1989 a nonprofit organization, the Arlington Partnership for Affordable Housing—APAH. The organization receives support from Arlington County, local churches, private donors and developers. Tom was the first president, who, in that capacity, got the organization off the ground. In the early days, our dining room table was the office until the financial foundation was secure enough to rent space. The Catholic Bishops' 1986 pastoral letter, *Economic Justice for All,* had been the inspiration for this undertaking. With each of four couples contributing 250 dollars we set out to raise money and buy up the properties that were going on the market and which could become very expensive new buildings. Our goal was to maintain the garden apartments which have been the base of affordable housing in Arlington, Virginia, particularly for workers in the service sector. It is a mustard seed story, starting with a dozen units and over the years moving into hundreds, with continued growth likely. Our initial steps were steeped in prayer, as was every step thereafter, and we continued to be surprised as one thing after another fell into place. Initially Tom was the visible face of APAH. County officials were confident of his experience and integrity—he had served on the county planning commission for a number of years—but *I* thought that mortgage lenders were reassured by his gentle demeanor. His concern that everyone have a decent, safe place to live grew out of his own love of home, a concept and a concrete reality of ultimate meaning for him.

> I will not enter my home
> Or get into my bed
> I will not give sleep to my eyes
> Or slumber to my eyelids
> Until I find a place for the Lord
> A dwelling place for the Mighty God of Jacob
> (Evening Prayer, Psalm 132)

And where does one locate such a dwelling? In every human person.

I sense how life-giving it is to remain engaged and caring about the larger concerns of our community. Concrete commitment is a way to realize more fully that we belong to something larger than our own sorrows or our own selves. The community in which I live is comprised not only of affluent government officials, but of new teachers, single mothers and the elderly on fixed incomes. They need homes and our community needs them. And are not these strangers part of the communion of saints?

October 4, 2003
Today is the feast of Saint Francis of Assisi. It was on this feast in 1977 that I began to work at the United States Conference of Catholic Bishops, as the first director of a new secretariat for the laity. It was both exciting and scary to enter the world of church official-dom, whose progressive pushes and pulls, as well as understandable resistance, seemed constantly in play. On my way to the entrance I paused to look at the statue of Christ, hand raised as in greeting, in front of headquarters at 1312 Massachusetts Avenue. At the base of the statue were the words, "I am the light of the world."

When the offices moved from downtown Washington to the neighborhood of Catholic University, the statue traveled across the city, and today remains a noticeable presence on Fourth Street, a bearer of memories and a reminder of stories.

Remembering

For twenty years I saw the statue almost every day, Christ greeting me and the other workers who tended to the church's business. Once a visiting German bishop whom I was escorting about the premises told me the scriptural citation was wrong. He pointed out that Jesus said "*You* are the light of the world," but I defended everything about the statue. Now I know that the light shines both ways, that both versions are scriptural, but then I was happy with the inscription the way it was. I needed the light that was Christ's. Let it be, I thought.

Even now, no longer an employee, I occasionally pass the statue and memories come coursing through my consciousness. People, places, situations, movements, historical currents, cultural shifts—they all form a framework of gratitude, and ignite a desire to understand how the pieces fit together, how we fit together, a desire to understand the nature of change. For change is what I'm grappling with now.

Remembering is the foundation of memoir which writer Patricia Hampl says is an effort to learn things one could not otherwise know; it is a movement toward talking about big issues, including meaning and values. Journal writing is one way to capture the flow of life, to touch the core of gratitude for what has been—not only personally but communally.

I was musing on these matters when Dana Greene, a historian and biographer, and a longtime friend, stopped by for coffee. She lives in Atlanta now, so we don't see each other with the regularity we used to enjoy. Dana has always had a sense of mission about larger things, and the challenge of breast cancer some years earlier only heightened that sense. A history professor for many years, she has been drawn to writing biographies of women (Evelyn Underhill and Maisie Ward are published, and she is currently researching poet Denise Levertov). She now believes her call is to bring together three passions: higher education that is hospitable (along the thinking of educator John Bennett) and community oriented; higher education that is intellectually excellent; and education that offers women the opportunity to excel. She wonders if a Catholic women's college might be the only place where these three passions can be expressed. And she wonders if she should pursue that idea. This led me to wonder where are the public spaces (aside from the academy) where women can meet and converse about matters of concern. I can't seem to locate any.

Tonight some friends gathered to remember Tom. One of the responsibilities of the living is to remember the dead. People recalled Tom's quiet personality, his suspenders (part of his normal dress in later years), the two pens he always clipped to his shirtfront, even when wearing a long sleeved, cuff-linked dress shirt. Others recalled his love of history, particularly biblical history, and everyone mentioned his acceptance of different others.

I find all this memorializing to be right for many reasons. Indeed, to remember is an ancient imperative, rooted in Judeo-Christian life. Every year through ritualistic remembering Jews lead their younger family members into the past, into their collective story of oppression and liberation: the Passover. The rubrics are pretty well established but once in a while a new strand appears which may trouble family elders.

Jewish Remembering

One Passover our family was invited to the Leibner household for a Seder celebration. The Leibners—grandparents, a great-uncle, and five members of the core family (including three teenage boys) warmly welcomed six Leckeys, including two boys and two girls—all teens. After the familiar Exodus readings, Judy, the mother of the household, took up *The Diary of Anne Frank*. Her mother—the grandmother—sprang to attention. "Something's wrong," she said in obvious alarm. One grandson Lincoln gently told his grandmother they would explain later. Judy continued with the Frank chronicle. Once again Grandmother demanded to know what was going on. Judy put down the book and with a suppressed cry said, "Mother, oppression is oppression whenever and wherever. Moses, Anne Frank ... it's similar." The reading continued but Grandmother was not convinced. Today she might be more open to her daughter's point of view since we know one of the great temptations of our time is to forget the Holocaust, or at least to diminish its importance in the life of the Jewish people and the world at large. Jews do well to remember.

Christian Remembering

The same can be said about Christians. Every Sunday the Catholic community gathers to remember the life, ministry, death and resurrection of Jesus of Nazareth, whom we believe to be God's own incarnation. Indeed the Mass is filled with remembrances, including remembrance of our dead: our ancestors in faith, early popes like Cletus and Linus, the martyrs Felicity, Cecilia and others. On Ash Wednesday the ministers intone words we may try to forget, but the church won't let us, "Remember, that you are dust and unto dust you shall return." Remembering is central to our identity. I don't know how I would live these days of change without remembering, not just the dead, but the way that life has been manifested and the way it continues to pulse through this land of the living.

Women's Remembering

Women have, over time and cultures, found creative ways of remembering their histories, both personal and communal. The American frontier required women to call on both courage and creativity in order to establish homes, and often simply to survive a variety of dangers. Frontier women performed a new art, that of quilt-making, and the quilting often contained a history of the family or of the community. Every time a baby died (and that was a frequent occurrence) the women of the community created patches for a quilt to be given to the grieving mother. Some of these quilts, the children's quilts, can be seen at the national Museum of American History in Washington, D.C. Churches figure prominently in the history of quilting, providing a gathering place for families and communities to tell their stories.

When the Catholic Bishops of the United States decided to write a pastoral letter about the concerns of women they began with a consultative process, one designed by women. Local churches facilitated the gathering of small groups of women who engaged in a form of structured conversation, much of which was recalling the women in their own lives who had influenced them—grandmothers, teachers,

political figures, saints—and extrapolated from *their* stories the qualities the women deemed important for their own self-direction.
While the pastoral letter was not passed by the assembly of bishops—
the only failed pastoral in the history of the United States Conference
of Catholic Bishops—there was widespread agreement that the
consultation process, with its storytelling and remembering, was very
successful.

October 8, 2003
This evening I went out to dinner with a small group of women who,
except for one, are all single. I noticed how I still feel very married, and
I wondered if Jesus knew what he was talking about saying there is no
marriage in heaven. At some point in a long marriage we become
aware of something like fusion. The single women had all been
divorced for a number of years. They've managed to raise teenagers on
their own, hold down jobs, construct satisfying social lives and find
ways to volunteer their skills to the wider community. They demon-
strate resilience. But there are differences in our experience.

October 9, 2003
Butler's Lives of the Saints notes that today is the feast of Dionysius the
Aeropagite about whom little is known definitively. It is believed,
however, that he was converted to Christianity by Saint Paul in
Athens. This bit of information led me to Paul's speech about the
unknown God (Acts 17:22–31) and I felt a measure of comfort in one
of my favorite lines, "In him we live and move and have our being." In
the speech Paul talks about the resurrection of the body, a difficult
concept for most Athenians and I imagine for most people through
the ages. But this idea keeps drawing me into deeper reflection. What
does it really mean? We have a book in our library which Tom read at
the time of his first heart attack in 1975. It is called *True Resurrection*
by H.A. Williams. I must begin a search for it.

After reading the Athenian speech I started a rosary, and the first mystery, the Annunciation, opened up a deep meditation. It began on the surface with flashbacks of meeting Tom on the feast, March 25, 1954. We were at an "opera party" where people sat in silence and listened attentively to operatic recordings. Years later Tom used to say that it was the perfect setting for a shy person like him. That particular night the opera was Verdi's *La Traviata*, and during our marriage we would listen to it once a year, usually on March 25. After some time of reverie the meditation moved into a stillness. I became aware that the angel who invaded Mary's life, was inviting her into a whole different world, and that difference turned Mary's world upside down. The miracle is that from that upside-downness, new life emerged. In the stillness I began to wonder if it were this totally different world that Tom was now exploring. He used to say that when he died he would be a quaver in the universe. A quaver in music is a trill whose sound never ends. I like that. Why? Perhaps because it suggests many possible forms that life everlasting may take. Our granddaughter Maria wrote a little essay in which she mentioned that her grandfather had died and the night after she noticed the curtain in her room billowing. She said to herself, "It's the quaver." Women who have cared for children in different stages of development have long recognized that in children, the veil between different realities is thin. Children have not yet built walls between themselves and "otherness."

A card from Dana arrived today, yellow roses in full bloom, with the message, "Good to find you in bloom and with gladness in your heart." She's right. There is gladness, but also sadness. The quavers are appreciated but I wish there were something more than ephemeral presence. There is really nothing like touching, holding, embracing a beloved person. To touch is human. It connects us, gives us a feeling. So I substitute things that were physically close to Tom; I wear his old sweaters, and read books he especially liked. I think of these "things" as ordinary sacramentals, and see in them traces of the humanly sacred.

October 11, 2003

I attended a bereavement workshop with a friend whose mother, Stella, died at age ninety-three, three months before Tom. I visited Stella every so often in the assisted living residence nearby. She eventually moved to the nursing floor and was bedfast. These visits revealed how, at the end of life, one thing after another is "given up." Shakespeare really knew what he was talking about when he described the world as a stage where we go from infancy to youth to middle years and to old age whence we find ourselves "sans teeth, sans eyes, sans taste, sans everything" (*As You Like It*). Today we might see Shakespeare's image in terms of moving: We leave our homes for assisted living, make choices about what few pieces of furniture, art and family photos we will keep with us. In the end we may have only our rosaries.

The poet Anne Porter, still writing at age ninety-five, says that the art of writing may be the only pursuit that old age can't wreck. When you can no longer sing (eyesight too dim to read the music) or drive (because your children have taken away the car keys), you can still write. I told a Jesuit friend about Porter's observations and he shared that his ninety-nine-year old mother who lives alone writes letters every Sunday afternoon. The letters simply describe the "now" moment, the sunlight in the garden, the sounds of a Sunday afternoon.

On one visit I found Stella agitated, trying to use a phone which didn't exist, believing she was in a hotel and needing to talk with the manager. We couldn't really converse so finally I stood up, touched her hand, and prayed a Hail Mary aloud. A great calm came over her and as I was leaving she cautioned me to be careful not to bump into the protruding wheelchair. She was a watchful mother again, still in the land of the living.

The bereavement workshop was a disappointment. The speaker was disorganized and seemed to make light of the grief people were expressing. Many were parents who had lost a child and the emptiness was swallowing them up. My friend and I left at noon.

October 17, 2003
Gathering my courage, I traded in Tom's Mini-Cooper sports car for a sedate and larger Toyota Camry, something suitable for a woman in my circumstances. It was an emotional letting go. The Cooper had such a central metaphorical place in Tom's funeral. The homilist ended his reflections with a riff on the old spiritual "Swing Low, Sweet Chariot," adding, "Tom, take your Mini-Cooper on home, swing low all the way."

I did all the trading and the buying on my own. A new experience for me—it was the sort of thing I never wanted to bother with—but within myself, I thought I heard Tom saying, "You're doing fine." I had considered bringing a male friend with me, someone knowledgeable about cars. I thought I would be taken more seriously with a man asking needed questions. But then I thought, "I can do this."

October 18, 2003
Kate Curry, a painter whom I've known for many years, came from California for a visit. Unable to attend Tom's funeral, she wanted a face-to-face connection. Usually she creates large dynamic paintings but sometimes makes her own paper for smaller, more detailed pictures.

I have several of her paintings, one an explosion of wild flowers on a mountain in the Pyrenees. It is on wood and is called "The First Mountain of Thomas Merton." The yellows stand out.

Our conversation traveled backward to our early years as young parents, when she was still married to Neal and our families shared holidays and attended political events together. When she and Neal divorced, many of their friends were saddened, myself among them. Her decision to move to California came after a thorough review of her life, almost chapter by chapter. Her daughter and family were on the West Coast, as were her sister and brother. Kate's father, Ralph, whom we all called Captain Curry because of his long service in the Coast Guard, was eighty-nine at the time, living nearby in Virginia. Kate had to convince him that he could do the things he loved— music and gardening—on the other side of the continent. It was the right decision; her work and life with her extended family have flourished. Captain Curry died happy in his new surroundings.

Kate is as she always has been: direct and forthcoming, always interested in others, always loving. To be with her is to receive an infusion of energy.

October 27, 2003
A quick trip to the dermatologist turned out to be the source of some needed counsel. The doctor offered this advice for me: patience. I'm trying to pay attention to that advice. Later, lunch with some women friends in a noisy restaurant brought forth confessions of hearing loss from all of us, amidst much hilarity. Laughter and friends. What could be better? Both draw us into the center of being human. All through these days and weeks and months friends have created a web that holds me securely. They do this by including me in their ordinary lives. They are the everyday saints and they offer a form of communion. People sometimes wonder if Jesus ever laughed. Of course he did. We know he wept, and both crying and laughter are signs of human life.

November 1—All Saints
Last night and again today I pondered something I heard long ago, namely that on All Hallows this world and the other world are closer. My own overall experience since Tom's death has been precisely that: There is an exchange, back and forth, between the living and the dead. This awareness is particularly vivid during evening prayer as a sense of presence with those who have died: my parents, friends, Tom. My "this world" friends are also there in some way. I really don't feel I'm praying alone.

Vespers for the Feast of All Saints—the people's feast—has this prayer: "We pray this day that the great cloud of witnesses support and encourage us as we make our way to you, and may we, one day, be united in the communion of saints."

Two huge Christian beliefs are coming to the forefront of life now: the communion of saints (and how large the cloud of witnesses is), and the resurrection of the body. They seem to me to be intertwined, although at this point, I'm not sure how.

November 6, 2003

The Woodstock forum on "Catholic Traditions of Peace and War" was finally held today. Theologians, ethicists, public policy experts, representatives of the media came together in dialogue to try to get a deeper understanding about what makes a war just. Naturally Iraq was on everyone's mind. So was Iran. Benedictine sister Joan Chittister moved the conversation toward women and war. "No amount of smart bombs or technological precision will reduce the cost of the way women go to war. When we wipe out an electrical grid that we call a military target we wipe out the food making capability of women in the entire area.... We must understand that women who as a class are never included in the decision making that leads us to war, must at least be included in the class that negotiates the peace."[3]

When we planned the forum we realized that peace-building was hardly touched upon. The Jesuits want a book to come out of this event that would address questions of peace-building. I'll be involved in bringing the book to life, something I'm grateful for because I'm more acutely aware now than ever that work is important for my sense of wholeness. Another reason is that this "Just War" project is good work, and good work is something everyone needs for a meaningful life. And this applies to women who do not work outside the home. Their work of making a home is laden with meaning. Some years ago, I read about the mental health of concentration camp survivors, and how men and women survived the ordeal. One writer found that men who previously derived meaning from going outside to work, and who could not do so in the camps fared worse than women who were basically trying to do the same thing they had always done, only in a different and more difficult setting: namely, to create a small place of beauty, provide whatever comfort was possible, gather whatever food was available. In other words, they tried to create a home, however meager it might be. The point is that whatever form it may take, work is one of the elements needed to safely navigate change.

November 11, 2003

This evening at the Washington opera with friends was soul-stirring. Last summer when these good friends invited me to join in making some cultural plans together, it was like water in the desert. I knew I would not shrivel up and die inside. I was right. The opera, Wagner's *Die Walküre*, was one of the more moving musical experiences of my life. Placido Domingo was magnificent, but then, so was everyone on stage. I felt like we were watching—no, *drawn into*—some deep, analytic experience where gods and mortals work through what "life on earth can be." This, too, has something to say to the "land of the living."

Reflecting on Art

One of the effects of loss and change is the swing between emotional numbness and rivers of sorrow. Immediately after Tom's death I was cautioned against watching television, and now I understand why. Our relationship to television is passive, but the arts offer something completely different. A stage play is multidimensional. The live people on stage and the live audience are interacting at some level. Music, which has been called the language of the soul, also interacts with our human rhythms. And paintings reveal to us the glory of light, and so open us to the light that fills the world. Art and other forms of culture seem especially important now, not only for individual emotional health, but for the health of our nation, whose soul is aching.

November 14, 2003

It was my turn this morning to lead the Woodstock seminar. We continue to study the documents of the Thirty-Fourth General Congregation of the Jesuits. My task was to unpack the Decree on Poverty, which I understood to be a caution against arrogance. It seemed to me that the real issue, not only for Jesuits but for all Christians, is detachment. Did Jesus not come for our liberty? How free can we be? How free do we want to be?

Reflecting on Freedom and Resurrection

Such questions (like those about freedom) are a way into the mystery of the resurrection. I look at it this way: We can be dead in any number of ways, long before the body dies. We can be intellectually dead, not letting in new ideas or new possibilities. We can be emotionally dead, letting love dry up. We can even be physically dead while still breathing: alienated from our bodies and our sexuality. All of these aspects of our being desperately need the new life of resurrection, and the way that resurrection happens will surely rise from our everyday lives and may not always be immediately recognizable.

Remember the resurrected Jesus? He was recognized in the ordinary actions of life: preparing food on the beach, eating with friends, walking and conversing with friends.

When our foremothers went to jail to secure the right to vote not only for themselves but for future generations, that was resurrection. When a battered wife finds the courage to leave an abusive situation, that's resurrection. When a woman in midlife decides to follow her dream of studying the violin, that's resurrection. When Elizabeth Ann Seton, Catherine McAuley and a host of founders of communities of women religious followed their inner voice that urged something new—that was resurrection. We need to sharpen our attentiveness to the signs of resurrection all around us, and within us. I know I need to do so.

November 18, 2003

My train trip to New Haven for a lecture at St. Thomas Catholic Center at Yale University was unexpectedly eventful. A young man in a wheelchair and his able-bodied traveling companion (a young woman) settled in across from me. Within minutes a film crew appeared and set up in front of them. During the trip from Washington, D.C., to New York City the young man, Dan, was the focus of a "train narrative," which I easily overheard.

The previous summer he, with his companion, traveled through Europe for the purpose of viewing art. Both are artists, he a portrait painter. During the course of several interviews the woman told of meeting Dan, who has cerebral palsy, at Towson State University Art School, liking him and, over time, learning his language. She is a careful interpreter.

It was clear that she respects him and admires his work, which they would be showing to an interested New York gallery. But more than that, there was a definite bond between them. At one point she fed Dan, then cleaned his mouth. It was all so natural, so much an act of tender friendship. Dan won an academy award for a short documentary about his life in which he played himself.

For days afterward, I was so aware of how wondrous the world is, and how I witnessed resurrected life on the train to New York City.

November 27, 2003—Thanksgiving

We gathered in Vermont for this first Thanksgiving without husband and father and grandfather. Our daughter Mary Kate and her family hosted her extended and still grieving family. I was placed at the head of the table like the matriarch.

Most of the family stayed in Mary Kate's large home except for me. I had a room at a nearby inn. I felt I needed the space, both psychological and emotional, and for that the inn was perfect. A good part of Thanksgiving morning was spent reading by the inn's fireplace.

When I arrived at the house the turkey was in the oven, the vegetables prepared, everything apparently under control. It had to be a collaborative effort because Mary Kate is so busy all the time engaged in her younger son's therapy. He has been diagnosed with a neurological developmental disorder, and the therapy requires his mother, father, and even his older brother to engage in "floor time" which means total attentiveness to Conor. This happens six times a day. The presence of cousins Monica and Grace took some of the pressure off. Children can often be the best guides for one another. Thanksgiving night we all sang a bit of "Alice's Restaurant" a meaningful moment for all of us since last year Tom sang and recited the whole of that American epic which was lots of fun. This year was fun too, although a bit more subdued. I think we were all thankful for one another, perhaps subconsciously in touch with the communion of saints.

November 29, 2003

Tommy drove me to Albany where I caught a train to Manhattan so I could meet friends for some pre-Christmas time in New York.

St. Patrick's Cathedral was beginning to look like Christmas with wreaths on the doors and garlands here and there. I wanted to go to the Lady Chapel where Tom and I were married on a warm June day so long ago, and I did. I sat in the chapel, alone. My choice. My friends offered to be there with me, but I needed to be in that space alone, with the calm statue of Our Lady. For the first time I noticed that the altarpiece is a ceramic rendering of the Annunciation. Sitting in that small, elegant chapel I decided *I will celebrate the feast of the Annunciation in 2004, the fiftieth anniversary of our meeting.* I decided in that moment to invite friends to join me at home for Vespers.

I looked to my right and saw the statue of the Pietà where Tom said he knelt in prayer before our wedding began, asking for the grace to be a good husband. He was twenty-three years old. "And not knowing what lies before you...." words from the old marriage rite.

On our way back to Washington we stopped by the Cloisters, part of the Metropolitan Museum of Art. The first time I entered this magical place was with Tom soon after we were engaged. He knew all about the unicorn tapestries and was my guide for that initial visit. There are seven tapestries and they are thought to be Belgian in origin. The overall theme of the tapestries is the fight between the unicorn (a mythical animal) and the humans who try to subdue it. The human hunters (in the sixth tapestry) manage to kill the unicorn, here thought to be the Christ figure. It is a shocking scene. The seventh tapestry has the unicorn once more, miraculously alive again. He rests chained to a wooden gate, a Christ figure perhaps (except that he's chained) which has been interpreted as Christ linked to humanity forever. There is another theory, however, that the unicorn is a symbol of the bridegroom secured by his lover. That's the version that Tom related to me a long time ago. It was consoling to see the unicorn in his usual place, a source of beauty for all ages.

Thoughts on Ordinary Time

It is almost Advent, a new beginning for the church year, a little over five months since Tom's death. What have I learned in this period of change and discovery? More than I can record.

Prayer has changed. Strange, but I do not pray to Jesus as much as I pray to Tom, a conversational kind of prayer. But more than that, prayer has taken on new depth and been the cause of new insight, not only or principally because of my own efforts at prayer, but because of a vivid awareness of the loving outreach of others who have supported my fragility with their prayers. I know that every prayer no matter how small or swift, every note, every phone call, every invitation—these together have formed a kind of prayerful net which holds me secure.

During Vespers all these loving gestures are there. I sense the joining of my praise and intercession with that of others, not only the dead (surely them) but also of the living who are enriching these changed days and weeks. Friendship has taken on an enlarged meaning, and Jesus' words, "I call you friends" carries a poignancy and promise.

The cemetery as sacred space is more than a notion, it is an experience. I go back and forth between home and grave carrying flowers and stones and little notes. It's like being at Jerusalem's Wailing Wall, a place to lean and to plead, connecting me to all the others who sorrow the world over.

Art and poetry and music are true nourishment, sources of strength while at the same time stirring some languishing emotions. They are life-giving. So is my current probing about various dimensions of resurrection. One point I feel convinced of is that our own resurrections are underway now, even as I write this.

Tracking the course of my days and nights through the medium of the journal has given me a mirror to see how grace and incarnation are at work in the most ordinary of circumstances, and alerting me to resurrections. It helps me to notice the great cloud of witnesses, living and dead, who are accompanying me on this mystery journey, for mystery it is.

MYSTERY TRIP

Each night, after he died

She'd take refuge in sleep

In the half-empty bed.

One hand caressed her rosary,

As if to fill, by wordless touch,

A corner of the chasm.

Her other hand held tight

A rock she'd found on a trip with him.

Flat, smooth, like a footprint,

It brought her comfort to hold it,

to let it lead her back

to a land of sweet, unbroken dreams,

or forward, on the mystery trip,

no way yet clear. [4]

FOOD FOR THOUGHT

1. How do you keep track of the graces flowing through your current life? Daily prayer? Spiritual direction or friendship? Journaling?
2. How would you describe the relationship between friendship and the communion of saints?
3. Have you found art (music, poetry, photography, painting, textiles) to be an opening to the sacred? What are your other experiences of the sacred in the ordinary?
4. How is remembering a way to better understand your life and the lives of others?

RITUAL

• Experiment with different forms of Evening Prayer (Vespers) at day's end. It may be as simple as playing some music or chant, and sitting quietly to listen. The companion CD to this series, *Called to Holiness*, offers some excellent choices. (There are inspiring arrangements of sung Vespers by Rachmaninoff and Palestrina; simpler versions are available from Weston Priory in Vermont. Musical forms of evening prayer can be especially helpful for those of us busy at day's end with meal preparation and other household matters.) If you have more discretionary time, experiment with different constructs of Evening Prayer. In chapter two, I will say more about the *Book of Morning and Evening Prayer* arranged by the Sisters of Mercy in Silver Spring, Maryland.

• There are other versions of Vespers especially suited to women available from monasteries of Benedictine Sisters, such as in St. Joseph, Minnesota, and also from the Grail in Loveland, Ohio, a movement of laywomen.

• Begin a journal to record your interaction with God; the journal can also elicit previously unexpressed insights and feelings.

CHAPTER TWO

• ADVENT, CHRISTMAS, EPIPHANY •

A Time of Transition and Trust

Entering Advent

There is a version of *Morning and Evening Prayer* developed by the Sisters of Mercy which, while in harmony with the official prayer of the church, is especially sensitive to the life and needs of women around the world. It is respectful of both the values of inclusive language and scriptural integrity. The translation of the psalms and canticles is that of the International Commission on English in the Liturgy (ICEL). I love this version of the church's prayer for many reasons, among them the structure which is that of the cathedral office (which predates and is different from the monastic office). The prayer book includes prayers and readings for feasts, both the well-known ones, and others less well-known but representative of countries outside Europe. For example on August 7, Saint Cayetano of Argentina is recognized as the patron saint of bread and labor. His intercession is sought on behalf of the world's hungry. The people of Argentina also honor Our Lady of Luzon on May 1. And on September 20, Saints Andrew and Paul of Korea are remembered as martyrs for the Christian faith. This fits with the mission of the Sisters of Mercy which is worldwide, and with the vision of this series on women's spirituality. The spiritual genius of Catherine McAuley, founder of the

Sisters of Mercy, clearly inspires this work of prayer. Her words introduce the Advent section: "To obtain recollection we must entertain a great love for silence."

Silence has a special place during Advent, a time of waiting and expectancy. Two women who are central to the unfolding Christmas story—Elizabeth and Mary—are themselves in a state of waiting: They are pregnant. And like women the world over, they are tuned to the hidden and silent life growing within them. The life cannot be hurried. Ripeness is everything, just as it is in every creative act. So is space. Musicians know the importance of rests in music; they help us savor what has gone before. Gardeners recognize that without empty space in the garden, the vegetables and flowers could become a jumble. Athletes attest to the necessity of rest intervals to replenish energy. Space and silence are woven into the creative dynamic. In closeness to unseen life, whatever its form, we draw closer to God. One prayer for Advent Vespers asks this: "As the moon and starts illuminate this night, we thank you for the gift of life and beg your protection for all you have made."

Entering into Advent of 2003, I prayed for both illumination and protection, all the while convinced that seeds of new life had already been planted. The feasts of this season contributed to the sense of wonder: Saint Nicholas, patron of children, on December 6, and Our Lady of Guadalupe on December 12. And, of course, Christmas Eve.

I was in New York City for the First Sunday of Advent and at Mass, the priest's homily stressed that Advent is a time of transition, a time between what was and what is to come. The words had a poignancy: "Time between" aptly described my feelings.

My personal Advent meditations began to focus on what was needed to be in touch with transition, and several qualities surfaced in these meditations: courage and trust, along with watchfulness, that is, being attentive to the stirrings and signs of life. Could it be possible, I wondered, that Resurrection and Advent are intertwined?

I found the Williams book I'd been looking for, *True Resurrection*, and it is all that I hoped for. I keep it close at hand. There I read that the experience of unity is an integral part of resurrection. I was struck rereading my journal entries by a growing sense of continuity and connectedness in prayer, in reflection, in simple human experience. If there are fewer journal entries for this cycle than for Ordinary Time that may be because I have been gaining more equilibrium, if only subconsciously.

In the early days of Advent I came across a poem by Anne Porter which I included in my Evening Prayer.

PROPHETS
Once in the Advent season
When I was walking down
A narrow street
I met a flock of children
Who all came running up to me
Saying that they were prophets
And for a penny they
Would prophesy
I gave them each a penny
They started out
By rummaging in trash-cans
Until they found
A ragged piece of silk
It's blue, they said
Blue is a holy color
Blue is the color that
The mountains are
When they are far away
They laid the rag
On a small fire
Of newspaper and shavings

And burned it in the street
They scraped up all the ashes
And with them decorated
Each other's faces
Then they ran back to me
And stood
In a circle 'round me
We stood that way
In a solemn silence
Until
One of the children spoke
It was the prophecy!
He said that long before
The pear tree blossoms
Or sparrows in the hedges
Begin to sing
A Child will be our King.[1]

Journal Entries

December 6, 2003—Feast of Saint Nicholas

Since returning home from New York, I've been trying to figure out how I would ritualize the evening meal during these days of Advent waiting. The Advent wreath seemed too much in this new state of solitude, so I tried a variation on the ancient custom. I lit a small votive light, placed it in the midst of a few sprigs of holly and said aloud the prayer I had recited since age thirteen.

"Hail and blessed be the hour and the moment in which the son of God was born of the most pure Virgin Mary, at midnight in Bethlehem in the piercing cold. In that hour, vouchsafe O my God, to hear my prayer, and grant my desires, through the merits of our Savior Jesus Christ and his blessed mother. Amen." Our family said this prayer at the lighting of the wreath each evening, and I said it many more times during the course of a day. With the children gone, Tom and I carried on the tradition, just the two of us. And after many decades of granted desires (some in unexpected ways) the prayer carries with it my deep trust. But this year something was wrong. The ritual seemed empty. The votive light did not convey the spirit of Advent. Finally, I unearthed our old advent circle, arranged the purple and rose candles, and reinstated the usual ritual. Once more I was explicitly connected to the larger church. But as I said my Advent prayer with the words "grant my desires," the question of intention remained. What do I desire of God at this time?

It is important to be honest when facing such a question. Jesus typically asked those seeking a cure, "What do you want?" It is not always easy to get to the root of desire. A reading from Vespers includes these words: "He will transform our lowly body that it may be conformed to the body of his glory...." (Phillippians 3:20–21) Perhaps I desire that transformation, but I should remember that Jesus' glorified body bore wounds, and so it is with us.

December 12, 2003—Our Lady of Guadalupe
In the new headquarters of the United States Conference of Catholic Bishops is a statue of Our Lady of Guadalupe that was hidden for years in the basement of the old building. It is a radiant work of art, small with vibrant colors and gold leaf; in some mysterious way, it carries a spirit of peace and hope. In this it reflects the description of Saint Juan Diego's vision of the "ever virgin, Holy Mary, mother of the God of Great Truth, Teori." She asked Juan Diego to go to the bishop of Mexico and request a church be built on the spot of her appearance. The bishop told him to come back another time. And so he returned to the site of the vision (Mount Tepeyac) and there had another long and loving conversation with Mary who once more sent him back to the bishop. This time the bishop said he must have a sign if he was to believe it was a true heavenly message. Mary told Juan Diego to gather flowers from the barren mountain, and he did, all kinds of beautiful flowers known only to faraway Castile in Spain. Mary then

placed the flowers in Juan Diego's rough cloak. When he arrived at the bishop's home the flowers fell to the ground and, much to the surprise of the bishop, Juan's cloak was imprinted with the image of the Virgin. Whether every detail of this story is factual has long been disputed, but what has not been disputed is the power of the story in the history of Central and Latin America to engender hope, especially among the poor. Our Lady of Guadalupe today is revered as the patron of the Americas, and is an inspiration to those advocates of the oppressed and marginalized. I think women everywhere have reason to be devoted to her.

December 14, 2003—Feast of Saint John of the Cross
This is an especially important day for me as I recall how, in his last years, Tom would quote the Carmelite saint: "In the evening of life only love matters." I brought a Christmas wreath to the cemetery today with the words of John of the Cross printed on a small card. I am reminded how indebted I am to John of the Cross, Teresa of Avila and all the Carmelites who through the centuries have shared the treasure of Carmelite spirituality, what I would call a practical (and poetic) mysticism.

December 21, 2003
Tommy came over this Sunday afternoon to hang a picture for me. His daughter Monica was with him and when the chore was finished she asked to stay. She helped me change the bed linen, and then we wrapped Christmas gifts. In midafternoon, we visited Betty, a resident in an assisted living facility. She is in her own small apartment and is always "up" to receive visitors, although she rarely ventures out of her apartment. Monica called her *Miss* Betty. It was striking to witness the instant rapport between an elderly person and a young child. They liked being with one another. When we left Betty, Monica and I walked through the public rooms and Monica noted that all the people were old, finally judging it "a good place" for them if they can't take

care of themselves. A certain wisdom flows through when we simply listen to children without feeling the need to be educators.

A Reflection on Love

Many years ago, I heard an Advent homily that spoke of the three times Jesus meets us in a special way. The first is the celebration of Christmas, including the days before when the whole world displays signs of anticipation with lights and greenery and festivities of all kinds. The second time is at the moment of our personal death when Christ receives us. The third is at the end of time as we know it, the Parousia, when Christ will come again uniting the cosmic order. The priest then dwelt on the first Christ encounter, at Christmastime, taking note of the depression that so many people feel at this time. He said that may be because the outward festive signs do not correspond to our inner feelings. His remedy was for each of us to reconcile the brokenness within so there is something for us to celebrate. That something is wholeness. That something is love, wherever we experience it. Miss Betty experiences the truth of John of the Cross. She knows how much love matters in the evening of life.

December 25, 2003—Christmas Night
I had been quietly dreading Christmas, especially Christmas Eve. In recent years, Tom and I relished the joy of simply being together before the busyness of Christmas day. He always filled a Christmas stocking for me, small treasures, repeated year after year. This year I feared I would be feeling sorry for myself. But Christmas Eve brought surprising grace.

Once again, children led the way. Monica was an angel in the early Christmas Eve Mass, so that solved the problem of when and where to go to church. The whole family gathered there, and afterward continued the celebration at Tommy's home. His wife, Margaret, had prepared a simple buffet, and most of the grandchildren, visiting for this first Christmas without their grandfather, had rehearsed

Christmas carols accompanied by various musical instruments. This musical offering was done with seriousness and skill—and obviously lots of practice. One of the glories of Christmas is music.

CHRISTMAS CONCERT

They made music—

children in white robes,

adults in formal dress,

the symphony with shining instruments.

The sounds washed over us,

winter pilgrims housed in the concert hall,

safe from the cold, dark artic air.

We sang of Jesus and his joy to the world;

Handel showed up with his sidekick Isaiah;

and, of course, Franz Gruber allowed us to sing together *Stille Nacht*

Two hours of beauty,

for the ear and eye,

and then we ventured back into the winter's dark and cold,

warmed by the music,

graced by the light of a Christmas star.[2]

Returning home and settling into my annual reading of the Christmas Eve section of Washington Irving's *Sketchbook*, I knew the hurdle of Christmas Eve without Tom had been overcome. One passage from Irving caught my attention:

There is an emanation from the heart in genuine hospitality which cannot be described but is immediately felt, and puts the stranger at once at his ease. I had not been seated many minutes by the comfortable hearth of the worthy old cavalier, before I found myself as much at home as if I had been one of the family.[3]

I read for quite a while and then started for bed. I was stunned to see a stocking hanging on the mantle, unnoticed during my reading time. After some hesitation, I emptied the contents so similar to other years: a hummingbird pin, a jar of jam, some pens—and the give-away—a copy of Tom Stoppard's play *Arcadia*, a favorite of my daughter Celia's. (I tried to read it once but it was much too complicated for me, jumping back and forth across time as it does). Obviously Celia had been at work between the Mass and the meal at her brother's. I went to sleep feeling surrounded by beatitude—the hospitality of family—which I had been reading about in the *Sketchbook*.

The next morning I was at peace, ready to prepare a Christmas meal for my family. At the end of the day, as everyone was heading out the door for their own homes, Tommy announced this year "a wonderful Christmas." And so it was.

But why? What made his holy holiday so rich for us? I think two forces were at work to make it so. One was the conscious exchange of love within the family; each of us was looking out for the others. The second was simply Christmas itself, an event so much larger than our personal lives. Christmas is Christmas and it carries itself.

Vespers begins during Christmas time with this greeting: "In the silence of night, God leapt from the heavens. Emmanuel, God with us! A child was born of the Virgin Mary. To us is born a Savior."

This Christmas my Amen is heartfelt.

December 31, 2003—New Year's Eve
The last day of the year in which Tom died. The whole world, at least the Western world, is merry at the thought of the passage of time. The end and the beginning, alpha and omega. And so with Tom. Is this the year when Tom's life began again? A life bathed in love and illumination? I try to see him, to sense him in the universe discovering the secrets of the way things are, a search that occupied him for his whole life. One Fordham Prep classmate wrote me at the time of his death that at age thirteen he was asking questions about the cosmos.

I am taking note of this holiday at our beach house, having driven here by myself two days ago, another "first" without him. Two weeks before his death we spent several wonderful June days here. The weather was slightly cool but bright with sunshine. Tom's mobility was limited, but nevertheless we drove to the far end of the boardwalk to enjoy lunch, watching some dolphins play, content to be in one another's company. One night we dined in an Irish restaurant and talked of being in Ireland for his next birthday when he would turn seventy. That, of course, did not come to pass. But it makes me wonder if I should journey there, for both of us.

It has been so long since I've written in this journal. My intent had been to do so each day. Perhaps life has been so full that the necessity of seeing each day in writing has been lessened. But I hope here in the quiet of the beach house (which is actually on a small lake) I'll do so, pausing to watch the gentle waterfowl: the Canada geese, mallards and the majestic grey heron suggestive of a bird version of Aslan, the lion king of the Narnia chronicles. It is time to savor simple pleasures. The journal can help me do that. It is a doorway to gratitude, and a reminder to trust.

January 1, 2004—New Year's Day
We also celebrate today the Feast of Mary, the Mother of God. The Vespers prayer (from the Sisters of Mercy) is like a link connecting women to one another. "Hear us this night, O God, as we pray on behalf of earth's women. May their wisdom, their suffering, their joy and their strength be inspiration for us so that we may meet each of life's events with courage and love. We place ourselves under the protection of Mary, your mother, who moved with grace through the events of her life. Through her intercession, we pray. Amen."

Whom do we count in the communion of saints? Surely the canonical saints, and surely our own beloved dead, all of them silently moving in and out of our daily lives. But there are the living, too. Known and unknown to us personally are those whose simple, ordinary lives give glory to God. I think of some Latina women I once tutored and whose stories included leaving their families behind to find work in the United States. They were so grateful to learn simple English phrases to enable them to navigate shops and taxis and hospital emergency rooms. I think of friends who drop everything to spontaneously minister to others—myself included—in time of need. I think of a retired doctor-friend who works several nights a week in a free clinic in my neighborhood. The communion of saints is a large arc, pulsing with life, and it spans time and eternity.

January 18, 2004
Martin Luther King, Jr., is remembered and honored this weekend. Some friends from my parish, including our pastor, came for dinner tonight. Minutes before they arrived, I heard the shocking news that Gene Sleevi, husband of Mary Lou Sleevi, a religious artist and poet, had died suddenly that morning. The Sleevis are friends of many years so I immediately called Mary Lou. Her words, "I miss him," cut right through the cracked portions of my own heart. Gene was an exuberant disciple of Vatican II, believing deeply in the call to lay leadership. And he was a partner in Mary Lou's artistic vocation, helping her frame and transport her large canvases of women in the Bible. I'll miss his gentle laughter, love of music and boundless enthusiasm. His conviction about the power of prayer taught me so much; I am forever in his debt.

January 23, 2004
It is now seven months since Tom's death. Mary Lou's words about Gene resonate with me: "I miss him." However, when I heed what I perceive to be Tom's urging that I pray in order to find and feel him, I'm comforted. I know he's right.

These days that follow Christmas—the time of Epiphany—have indeed held moments of revelation. Vespers for Epiphany includes Psalm 27 with these lines:

Deep within me a voice says,
"Look for the face of God"
So I look for your face,
I beg you not to hide.
Do not shut me out in anger,
Help me instead.
The psalm ends with these lines:
"Trust in the Lord. Be strong.
Be brave. Trust in the Lord."

I put these pieces of wisdom together with the intuitive (and experiential) knowledge that prayer brings us into the presence of God where, in fact, the dead inhere. Trusting in the presence we can freely offer the intercessions for Epiphany among them these prayers:

We seek an open heart, ready to respond to your inspirations;
we seek a desire for prayer; we seek the gifts of adoration and
wonder.

These prayers seem authentically rooted in the communion of saints. They lead into deeper trust.

January 28, 2004

I've sent Tom's desk, which was his mother's, off to Vermont to our daughter Mary Kate. We always intended that she would have it someday, but we never really factored in that death might be the decisive event determining when it would go. Even though I knew it was the right thing to do—an inspiration?—I felt chilled watching the movers, as if I were sealing my fate, and his, never to return.

Earlier in the day, I had read a passage from *Alain on Happiness* by Alain, an early twentieth-century French philosopher-journalist whose short observations on the human condition are always insightful. He says we bring flowers to the cemetery in order to bring our thoughts toward the dead that we may start a conversation with them.

Since the course of our thoughts depends principally on what we see, hear and touch, it makes sense to arrange ceremonies to stimulate the conversation. He goes on, "The dead are not dead; that is clear enough since we are alive. The dead speak, think, and act; they can advise, desire, approve, criticize; that is all quite true, but one must understand in what sense. All these things are in us; all are very much alive in us.... It is perfectly reasonable to ask oneself what it is that the dead wish."[4]

Theological Ruminations

Not only did I feel affirmed by Alain regarding my frequent conversations with Tom, and affirmed in the decision to begin rearranging the room that had been Tom's "day room" where he often read, worked on finances, or did some private writing at his mother's desk—but Alain laid out the theological notion of coinherence in a different and accessible language.

Coinherence, an ancient concept, refers to the Trinity and the mutual indwelling of the three Persons. Some early theologians spoke of each Person *belonging* to the others, or of the omnipresent God permeating the universe. Carrying the concept further one can imagine all of us belonging to one another, as in the communion of saints, and all abiding in God. Alain has not only enriched the concept of the communion of saints, he has given me another opening to ponder the meaning of resurrection.

January 31, 2004

Plans are proceeding to celebrate the feast of the Annunciation in March. It will be the fiftieth anniversary of the day I met Tom. In St. Patrick's Cathedral before Christmas, I made the decision to do so, and now is the time to begin implementing the decision. I met with caterers yesterday, a husband and wife, who are not only wonderful cooks, but sensitive people who seem to understand how important this March ritual is to me. The next step is invitations. When I was at St. Patrick's Cathedral before Christmas, I bought postcards depicting the Annunciation altarpiece in the Lady Chapel. They will serve as invitations.

February 11, 2004

A bed has been delivered to the "day room" transforming it into a proper guest room. Tom would approve. He always wanted our home to be open to others.

Today is the feast of Our Lady of Lourdes, and in the late afternoon, I received a phone call from Father Jude Siciliano, prior of the North Carolina Dominicans, with the news that Jim Campbell, O.P., had died one hour before. Jim was a friend of many years, a most interesting but restless soul, a born mendicant. Prior to joining the Dominicans he had briefly been a Trappist, and silence remained central in his prayer and behavior. For many years he was a Zen practitioner. As a Dominican his missions were many and varied from being an itinerant preacher in Africa, to an AIDS hospital chaplain in Tennessee, to a pastoral presence with migrant workers. One time in Honduras he was run over by a bus, an incident that tore all the flesh from one of his legs. The local doctors wanted to amputate the leg, but Jim's Dominican brethren would not give permission and instead arranged for him to be flown to Miami where, over the course of a year, his leg was rebuilt and he learned to walk again. He came through that ordeal beautifully, all the more remarkable since for years he had suffered from clinical depression. If one were to try to sum up Jim's life it would be to say that he suffered both internally and externally. Beyond clinical depression he also knew the spiritual desolation of the dark night of the soul. Maybe that's why he continually chose to be with those who also suffered. How fitting that he died on a feast day associated with healing.

February 14, 2004—Saint Valentine's Day

Like Christmas this was a holiday I had been dreading, and once again it was better than I expected. Peace came from the kindness of

Tom's brother Jay and his wife, Myra, who journeyed from New York City to spend the weekend with me. With maps spread out everywhere we planned our May trip to Ireland, a trip to fulfill a plan sketched out by Tom and me. All weekend in the back of my mind was Alain's point that the dead are still very much alive, desiring, approving and guiding.

Thoughts on Resurrection

Alain presents one way in which the dead are still alive, but understanding the meaning of resurrection does not stop at that point. Frederick Crowe, S.J., brings forth a fresh and, to my mind, exciting analysis of what the risen life is. In a paper titled "Complacency and Concern in the Risen Life," Crowe, who is at the Bernard Lonergan Research Center in Toronto, Canada, rethinks the resurrection which involves getting hold of the radical meaning of "is," namely realizing that the past—*all* the past—is present to God. All things are alive in God.

To elaborate his point Crowe uses the language of Psalm 89 which is about the span of life: "Seventy is the sum of our years / eighty if we are strong" and asks us to think with imagination backward over the seventy years of our life to the *beginning* instead of forward to death and burial. (He is using the number seventy for the totality of a life). The soul, writes Crowe, is our formal unity, giving us identity and wholeness. In life on earth the soul exercises its role in the present moment; in eternity it does so over the whole expanse of seventy years (or a lifetime). He goes on to say that in the resurrection the soul takes possession of the body as it is in God's presence, in the totality, the summation of its life. Crowe's exciting insight is that the soul does not leave the body at all, it leaves the corpse. The corpse and the body are different.

Like others whom I have been reading on the topic of resurrection, he asserts that life after death is in continuity with human life before death. Using the metaphor of a building he contends that life now is not the scaffolding, but the building itself going up brick by brick. We construct the building of our life, piece by piece, choice by choice.

And after death, in "the risen state," we are alive, but alive with a new consciousness deriving from the vision of God. Consciousness in the risen life goes beyond earthly consciousness but does not interfere with or destroy earthly consciousness. Rather it preserves its relevant features and properties and carries them forward to a fuller realization within a richer context. Nothing of what *is* is lost. It is not lost to God, nor to us. This does not mean that we do not experience loss. Of course we know loss in the present moment, but nothing is ever lost in an absolute sense.

Crowe underscores that we cannot change our past experience, but we can reflect on it, learn from it, and understand its meaning. Reflection is key. What we want to do is admit into consciousness the whole reality of our span of years, and admit the universe, too, with all its chaos and troubles. Yet Crowe points out that the real challenge for most of us is to accept our own selves and our own situation and our own involvement in the universe.[5]

In reading Crowe's paper, I was reminded of a story about the French Benedictine Jean LeClerc. The story was related by a woman who was well into her nineties (and has since died). She, a Protestant, and Father LeClerc were members of an ecumenical spirituality group and at one meeting she approached Father LeClerc and said that if he did not travel so much she would ask him to be her spiritual director. He replied: "If I were your spiritual director I would tell you there are only two things you need to know. The first is *accept yourself.* The second is, *Christ is risen.* That is the whole substance of my spiritual direction." She, widowed twice, told me that these words have been the foundation of her long life; she also said accepting herself is a life-long project.

February 24, 2004

Drew Christiansen, S.J., was in Washington for a conference and we shared a Shrove Tuesday dinner together. It was our first real conversation since Tom's death. Drew has been an important person to me ever since I made the Spiritual Exercises of Saint Ignatius with him many years ago. That was surely a time of epiphany, of self-acceptance and understanding, of building some sturdy parts of my life-house, and finding out where the weak and shabby parts are.

And now on the eve of Lent I'm hoping for clarification regarding my true desires. *What do you want?* Jesus asks, as he has always done.

Further Reflections on Advent, Christmas, Epiphany

This point in time, between Epiphany and Lent seems suited for some summary reflection and resolve. The fewer and shorter journal entries signal, I believe, a change in my inner world. I am not so much searching for points of meaning in daily life, as *living* them. Routines and daily rhythms are deepening a sense of trust, and there are simple and available structures for doing so. Vespers is a big one. Whether or not I'm "in the mood" I find that the simple ritual I've constructed around the Prayer of the Church is a source of strength and hope. The prayer and ritual can go on regardless of how I feel. Reviewing my journal entries to date I see how daily encounters with others are a source of wisdom. One example is my dermatologist, whose unsought counsel to be "patient" caught my attention. Discovering Anne Porter's poetry is another.

Advent especially has underscored the inevitability of transition throughout our lives. To live is to change. My transition to daily life lived alone has highlighted the need to embrace reality, to embrace the only life I have now. And with the now I see the connectedness between all that has been, all that is, all that will be. The freedom of now lies in my choices. While I am still puzzling over what I now really desire of God, I believe it will become clearer with patience and trust. And what does God hope for me? That question was central when I made the Spiritual Exercises.

FOOD FOR THOUGHT

1. What transitions in your life do you remember? How did they change your pattern of living, if at all? Could you describe any one of them as a "conversion"?

2. Remembering that nothing is ever lost in an absolute sense, imagine the construction of your life from its beginning to the present, bit by bit and choice by choice. Some pieces of the building may be marred or scarred, but it is a unique construction, lasting forever.

3. Ponder the distinction between a corpse and a body as Frederick Crowe describes it.

RITUAL

- Seasonal changes often occasion particular rituals and prayers. As days shorten, and darkness lengthens at the beginning of Advent, light some candles with deliberateness one or two evenings a week, alone or with others. The Advent wreath, an ancient custom, is a traditional way to do so. Invite a child or two (perhaps a grandchild) and an elderly friend to join in the candle lighting, the reading of Advent psalms, and an Advent poem. Then toast the evening star which is beginning to appear in the night sky with a glass of wine or juice, and play some welcoming music as a simple meal is prepared. The key to this ritual is to proceed in an unhurried fashion, which is the opposite of the commercial aspects of the season.

CHAPTER THREE

• LENT AND EASTER •

A Time of Renewal and Creativity

Welcoming Lent

Many years ago when my spiritual director greeted me on Ash Wednesday with the words "Happy Lent" I was puzzled. Whatever could he be talking about? Happiness and Lent did not fit together in my traditional and fixed idea about what Lent is and how I should act during the forty days. But the wise and experienced monk spoke of springtime; Lent occurs on the edge of spring, he said, a time of renewed life after a period of dormancy. That conversation has been very present to me during the days and weeks of this particular Lent.

A homily heard long ago also came to mind. The homily began with the question, "Have you ever thought of Lent as the season of love?" At the time *I* had not. The homilist had, and Robert Morneau, bishop and writer, certainly has. In his book of lenten meditations (*Ashes to Easter*) he introduces George Herbert's justly famous poem *Love* as a focus for reflection during the first week of Lent.

LOVE (III)

Love bade me welcome; yet my soul drew back,
Guilty of dust and sin.
But Quick-ey'd Love, observing me grow slack
From my first entrance in,

Drew nearer to me, sweetly questioning,

If I lack'd anything.

A guest, I answer'd, worthy to be here:

Love said, You shall be he.

I the unkind, ungrateful? Ah my dear,

I cannot look on thee.

Love took my hand, and smiling did reply,

Who made the eyes but I?

Truth Lord, but I have marr'd them: let my shame

Go where it doth deserve.

And know you not, says Love, who bore the blame?

My dear, then I will serve.

You must sit down, says Love, and taste my meat:

So I did sit and eat.[1]

Morneau points out that the "quick-eyed Love" longs for communion with all of us—no matter what.

For Ash Wednesday he writes, "The great questions of life deal with our finitude, our guilt, our anxiety, our death. These must be courageously and vigorously addressed."[2] They are the questions to be struggled with in Lent. And struggle it is. But remembering that love is endlessly solicitous helps the inner work, and helps our perseverance in facing such great questions.

Journal Entries

February 25, 2004—Ash Wednesday

Georgetown University's Dahlgren Chapel visually invited everyone who entered that sacred space to "come away" and discover how renewal happens. Vases held bare branches, and there were mounds of stones in the sanctuary, reminders of how beautiful starkness can be. I had a flashback to a lenten evening at Holy Cross Abbey, the Trappist monastery in Berryville, Virginia. It was dusk with a gentle rain falling. On my way to the chapel for Compline, I saw a small herd of cattle, black angus, grazing in the wet evening, and their silhouettes looked so beautiful against the gray night. Bare branches and dark silhouettes signal that beauty can exist in shades of gray. "One does not become enlightened by imagining figures of light, but by making the darkness conscious" wrote the psychologist Carl Jung.[3]

The rest of this first week of Lent is centered on a new and completely different project for me: preparation for the IRS submission. Tax preparation was Tom's *joyful* responsibility. He was good at it and he enjoyed it. He even enjoyed *paying* taxes, figuring that as a citizen he got a fair return for the payment. For me this kind of organizing of information is like learning a new language, and I'm looking for some sort of a code that will unlock the mystery. All I'm finding, though, is tedium and anxiety. I'm counting on the tax expert recommended to me by a friend to calm the troubled waters.

Ten years ago, we spent Lent at the ecumenical theological center, Tantur, located approximately two miles from Jerusalem and two miles from Bethlehem. On the first Sunday of Lent a small group from our sabbatical class decided to hike to an Orthodox monastery built on a hillside in the Judean desert in the vicinity of the Wadi Kelt, and then to continue the hike down to Jericho. This was an all-day adventure with Mass celebrated on a rocky promenade in the desert. We walked along narrow ledges, and there was a sense of danger with every step. The abiding feeling of that particular experience is that we had to depend on one another to move safely through the terrain. And isn't that what we have to do in the course of our life's journey? Community is not a luxury; it is a necessity.

March 3, 2004

Tom's brother Jay called from New York City with two pieces of news. The first was that he and his wife, Myra, purchased their plane tickets for our trip to Ireland in May. The other news was that Tom and Jay's sister, MJ, had died the night before: colon cancer which had spread to her lungs and brain. I was stunned because that night, the night she died, I dreamed of her. In my dream she was standing on a coffee table which Tom had made when we were first married. (The legs were not spaced properly so the table had always been unsteady; we had to be careful around it.) There were people surrounding MJ as she stood poised on the table. They looked worried about her being in such a precarious place. I took her hand and somehow led her off the table. Then we went into the hall where there were photos of my children. She looked at Tommy and Colum and said, "You have handsome sons." I replied, "So do you." She looked at me, said nothing, and then started up the staircase to the bedrooms. I knew, and she knew, that she was going to sleep. I went back into the main room where everyone was on edge not knowing what she might do upstairs. Soon, however, we knew she was asleep and everyone relaxed.

MJ, like most of us, could be difficult at times; in her case it was magnified by some deep personal sadness that caused alienation from those closest to her. This dream was consoling to me for several reasons. One was the sense that at last she was at peace with herself and with others, and it was yet another reminder that the dead are not all that far from us, ever.

March 8, 2004
Several priests from All Hallows College in Dublin are in the neighboring parish for a few days, meeting with some of us on a committee we call "Friends of All Hallows." Our purpose is pretty straightforward, namely to figure out ways to raise money for the college which is now principally a ministry center. Once it trained the priests who were missionaries to English-speaking countries like the United States. Now, the students are largely laity while priests use the beautiful facilities for retreats and renewal. I came to know the college in 1996 when I taught a summer course there. My class included lay ministers and theologians from South Africa and New Zealand, as well as England and Ireland, all of whom were not only competent but

also confident in a good way. All Hallows clearly has the potential for being a resource for the universal church as the face of ministry changes. But raising money? That's difficult even for well-known institutions. A little-known Irish college will need a large dose of creativity. Nevertheless, I look forward to these meetings, which are always fun. The conversation is lively with never a clear ending; rather the expectation is that more can and will be said later on which might be months later. It's a bit like being in an Irish pub where talking is highly valued. I've asked the priests to help me get tickets for the Abbey Theater in Dublin when I arrive there in May, and they've promised to do so.

March 14, 2004

My son Tommy and his wife, Margaret, had an early St. Patrick's Day dinner—corned beef, beautiful small boiled potatoes topped with bright green chopped parsley and, after dinner, Irish coffee and music. Tommy on the guitar and Margaret on the flute (with little Grace keeping the beat with an instrument unfamiliar to me) rendered "The Ould Orange Flute," one of Tom's favorites. It's really the story of his heritage. A Belfast man marries a "papist" from the south of Ireland, and the orange flute can't stop playing anti-papal songs. That describes Tom's parents, very much in love, and very much torn apart by the "Irish troubles," a gentle euphemism for the political violence that existed for so long.

March must be the season of dreams, because during the course of the evening, both Celia and Tommy shared recent dreams about their father. Celia's dream had him in a distant room, wearing medals and a kilt, with his arms extended as in welcome, and reciting a line from Lewis Carroll's "Jabberwocky": "Come to my arms my beamish boy (girl)."

Tommy's dream was set in a meeting room where he was seated at a long table with a lot of serious-looking people whom he thought might be accountants. Then a shadowy figure appeared—his Dad. He wanted to turn to the person next to him to say, "Do you see him?" but his Dad put a finger to his lips. "Shh" he said, and then drifted away.

March 15, 2004

On the ides of March, I finally went for my annual physical, except this one is several years late. With so much time spent in doctors' offices in the last few years, accompanying Tom to his internist and cardiologist, I have become hugely resistant to the medical world, a totally irrational reaction, I know. Only a friend's urging got me to make and keep the appointment.

My doctor ordered a series of tests which took two full days to complete. The results were normal. I've come to the conclusion that the symptoms I described to her have been the result of anxiety, what I've identified as "broken heart syndrome." My challenge at the moment is to think of my doctor as my friend and not as a necessary annoyance. This may require a true conversion on my part.

March 21, 2004

A weekend trip to Cumberland Gap in Tennessee to visit my son Colum and his family was fruitful for many reasons. The time spent in travel and visiting was peaceful. I think what was most precious was the time Colum and I had together, driving back and forth to the Knoxville airport. I saw my first blossoming trees of springtime along the route. Time alone in cars can be opportunities for deep sharing and we did some of that. I had a clear sense that Colum is happy in his teaching, with several extra projects in mind: for example, a trip for Appalachian college students to visit several cities of Eastern Europe so they can have on-the-ground experiences of different cultures. These extra possibilities enrich his work. The whole family seems to be thriving in the beauty and simplicity of those Appalachian hills, and that I count as blessing.

March 25, 2004—Feast of the Annunciation
Fifty years ago today, Tom and I met, and today I celebrated the event with family and friends, as planned last Advent, while praying in St. Patrick's Cathedral. With delicious food, champagne and a cake baked by our daughter Celia the celebration was truly a "high tea."

It's cherry blossom time in Washington so I splurged and found branches of pink and white blossoms for sale in a small florist shop, which reminded us all of creation's beauty. At 6 PM we prayed a version of Vespers, a version created for the occasion. This included the Angelus, Psalm 138 (one of our favorites), some Annunciation poetry, and a sung Magnificat. One of my favorite Annunciation poems is by Anna Kamienska, a Polish poet, who describes the emptiness we often feel when something wonderful disappears like an angel.

I am very glad I carried through with this ritual. For one thing, concentration on the feast reminded me of writer George Steiner's comment about the Annunciation, namely, that a visitation from the unseen world does more than rearrange the furniture of our life. Rather, if the wing beats (Steiner's words) are properly heard; *all* is transformed. Life is never the same. It seems to me that a loss can be a form of annunciation with the possibility—no, probability—of new life. That can happen in large and small ways.

When the Taliban first came to the ascendancy in Afghanistan I read about women in Kabul who were able to work in a United Nations–sponsored bakery. Everyone was very poor and very worn down from years of Soviet occupation. The women of the bakery worked for pennies each day but they were filled with gratitude. Why? There was no work, many suffered from injuries sustained in the war; there was no fuel, and the winter was bitter cold. But the women were warm when they baked, and they could bring bread home at the end of the day. Their children would not starve, at least not then. The women saw the establishment of the bakery as a kind of salvation, what I would call annunciation. So much had been lost to them, but the bakery was life-giving. As I read those accounts, I imagined the women bringing the bread home, like Eucharist. Truly there are many faces of eucharistic love, and the Afghan women's are among them.

St. Mary's College, Notre Dame
March 31, 2004

I arrived at St. Mary's College yesterday, right in the middle of Lent, for a one-month sabbatical. St. Mary's Spirituality Center arranged for this extended visit, but I wonder if maybe I am pushing "getting on with life" a little too soon, a little too far. My concerns were answered to some degree by a gracious St. Mary's welcome. I've been given an apartment in a dormitory, and the young women who live here are treating me with all the deference they show to grandmothers. A major practical concern is finding my way around the campus and observing the protocols of campus life. The students are helpful in this regard. Tomorrow I get a car which will give me a little more freedom. I'll be able to do some grocery shopping so not every meal need be taken in the student cafeteria.

The official title for my visit is "writer in residence;" it follows that there should be a writing project. And there is. This is the perfect place to do some necessary research for a book on the history and implementation of the Second Vatican Council's *Decree on the Laity*, which I've agreed to write.

As I settle into the sabbatical mode, I'm thinking again about the Tantur and Jerusalem sabbatical ten years ago. Tom was with me, which made it an emotionally stable, as well as intriguing experience. Driving to Tantur from Tel Aviv the night we arrived in Israel was magical, the darkness punctuated by different kinds of lights: stars, a bright moon and candles on the hillsides. The candles, I learned, belonged to groups of demonstrators, settlers mostly, who were objecting to actions of the Israeli government. I soon learned that most public acts had a political side.

Very early the next morning, I was lying on my bed when I heard the Muslim call to prayer, the first of many over the next few months. They always caused a pause within me, and a turn toward God.

There will be no such call here at St. Mary's, but there are many opportunities to experience something new, intellectually and spiritually. I am wondering, though, how I will handle the aloneness without my usual supports, simple everyday things like phone calls and mail, and social contacts with friends. Research is lonely under the best of circumstances, and my particular situation may emphasize that condition even more. Can I handle all this solitude?

April 2, 2004
Sister Kathleen Dolphin (director of the Spirituality Center at St. Mary's) and I paid a visit to the University of Notre Dame library where we were shown the latest technology for locating resources, which could be most useful for my work. As we witnessed the wonders of instant retrieval, someone mentioned it was like talking to God who knows all. You certainly could get that feeling.

I've been attending daily Mass at the Loretto Chapel on campus. Yesterday the First Reading was about Abraham being called by God to undertake a major change in his life—at age ninety-nine. The psalm antiphon was "If today you hear his voice, harden not your heart," even if you are ninety-nine—or seventy-one, as I will be in a few weeks. Forty years ago when I had just begun to pray the psalms in my daily life, I spent time meditating on that particular antiphon. Those forty years have been filled with so much life, with so much *choosing* life. The priest used Abraham's call to emphasize the inner meaning of life. He told a Sufi parable about people asking a spiritual master if there is life after death. The master laughed every time the question was asked. The people kept asking and the master kept laughing. Finally the master asked his inquisitors another question: "Is there life now? Are *you* alive?" The point of the questioning (and the laughing) is this: Live now. Let tomorrow take care of itself. I looked around at the Holy Cross Sisters in attendance, most of them elderly, their faces so brave and beautiful. They know about living in the present moment.

April 4, 2004—Palm Sunday
The liturgy in Loretto Chapel was memorable with the Passion of Christ read by four different people, one of whom was the celebrant. The others were two Holy Cross Sisters and a layman, signs of an inclusive liturgical life and community.

April 8, 2004—Holy Thursday
Today I flew home for the Easter weekend as planned. It feels so good to be among the familiar. I began observance of the Holy Days with the Nova Community, an intentional Catholic community started in 1968, for the purpose of implementing liturgical changes. It wasn't long, however, before issues of social justice shared the center of the community's concern. And while I haven't been a member for decades, I try to attend a Mass or prayer service with that community once or twice a year. The Holy Thursday service itself was both centered and reverent. From the foot washing to the recounting of Scripture, to the spoken prayers, what was evident was commitment to shared leadership. Seeing old friends was an added plus.

April 10, 2004—Holy Saturday
I saw my spiritual director this morning, which was an anniversary of sorts for us. Twenty-five years ago on Holy Saturday, we had our first meeting. Then he was simply a monk of the Abbey and a teacher in the school. Since then our relationship has grown into deep friendship largely because when I am with him I feel completely understood. And now he is the abbot, with many responsibilities. We hadn't seen each other since the previous August so there was much to discuss. He thinks my peregrinations (St. Mary's and soon Ireland) are good, a sign of choosing life.

Afterward I went to the cemetery, which is something Tom and

I used to do on Holy Saturday. Sometimes we went to Arlington National Cemetery, which can be a walk through American history.

April 12, 2004—My Birthday
I was to fly back to South Bend today but my flight was cancelled because of the heavy rains. The family marked the passage of another year of my life, yesterday, Easter. We read a George Herbert poem before the cake was cut.

EASTER
I got me flowers to strew Thy way
I got me boughs off many a tree
But Thou wast up by break of day,
And brought'st Thy sweets along with Thee.
Yet though my flowers be lost, they say
A heart can never come too late;
Teach it to sing Thy praise this day,
And then this day my life shall date. [4]

I think God is teaching my heart to sing even though sometimes it's hard to detect.

April 18, 2004
I've been back at St. Mary's for five days, obviously more settled than when I first arrived, with no excuses for not accomplishing something.

I awoke from a dream about Tom and me. We were in a house and music could be heard. He took my hand and we began to dance, and then he led me into a bedroom where we lay side by side, fully clothed, holding each other close. It felt so good. I said to him, "It doesn't get much better than this." Somehow I knew that our children were there, out of sight, but I could hear them happily racing through other rooms. When I stood up I realized we were in a basement room. I looked around and thought this is a fine space that can be rehabili-tated, brought to life. Tom and I will do this together, I said, and it will benefit the whole family. We'll start with new windows, casement windows that can open to the world.

All this morning I had a sense of refreshment, which pointed to something new on the horizon. Perhaps it was the dream or perhaps it is my decision to return home a few days earlier than originally planned. I realize I need my connections; that's clear now.

Reflecting on Dreams

Literature is filled with the power of dreams. Biblical literature, in a way, begins with Adam's dream—at least God casts Adam into a deep sleep and when he awakes there is a companion present to him: woman, "bone of my bone and flesh of my flesh." Did Adam dream? Did he dream of woman? Who knows? It's possible because now, thanks to modern psychology, we know that dreams often free our creativity, open up realms of possibility and contribute to the depth of our spiritual life.

Throughout the Hebrew and Christian scriptural texts dreams guide human action, provide insight and often help us to face life with courage and hope. Of particular poignancy for Christians is the dream of Joseph of Nazareth in which his fears about Mary's pregnancy are calmed. From that moment of trust in the ways of God, Joseph is part of the unfolding drama of Jesus.

Years ago, I was at a meeting with Morton Kelsey, an Episcopalian priest and a Jungian psychoanalyst who wrote many books on the spiritual life. I sat next to him for most of the weekend, so it was easy for me to see how he took notes. He used a lined copy book and wrote in the tiniest of scripts, filling the spaces between the lines. At some point I commented on his full notebook, and with a merry laugh he told me that he had hundreds of books like that, perhaps thousands. Most of them, he said, were filled with his dreams. Every morning, as soon as he awoke, he would begin to write. This raw material from his unconscious became the data for his ongoing prayer and spiritual reflection. He explained how the unconscious is not "veiled" before God, but is much more a direct experience of the Spirit, somewhat like the process of "awake" contemplation. He advised that I begin the practice of recording my dreams. I took the suggestion seriously not only because of his professional reputation but because of the person I saw before me, and the words he spoke to me and to others. His entire attitude toward that small ecumenical community which met regularly to search for common spiritual ground was one of humility. Morton was an authentically transparent personality, almost childlike in his innocent presence.

Off and on over the years, I followed his suggestion. I kept pencil and paper next to my bed and at certain times immediately upon waking, I made the effort to record dreams. The first lines of morning writing were illegible but as I persisted, the writing became clearer and I began to feel lighter. There was the sense that a part of my soul was opening and the resulting freedom allowed me to try new ways of being, new ways of praying and extended horizons of loving.

I believe dreams are loving contacts with the Divine.

April 22, 2004
Tonight was the twentieth Madeleva Lecture, an annual St. Mary's event that focuses on some aspect of women's spirituality. It is named for Sister Madeleva, a past president of St. Mary's and a well-known poet. It was she who opened the door for women to study theology at the graduate level.[5]

"Women Shaping Theology" was this evening's topic. Mary Ann Hinsdale, I.H.M., opened her lecture with a song. One of the valuable aspects of the annual lecture is the bringing together of different generations of women: students from St. Mary's, alumnae, faculty and friends. There are men in the audience, of course, but the range of women's ages and interests is notable. It makes me wonder if parishes might experiment with gathering women from different generations to share life and faith in the twenty-first century.

April 23, 2004

Ten months since Tom left for—God? To be a quaver? Ten months of missing him, trying to see his face, hear his laughter. On my way to early Mass today, I first heard, and then saw, two Canada geese, a *couple*, beginning their flight together. I took it as a sign that we are still going somewhere.

One of my favorite books is by the Nobelist Konrad Lorenz. It is a reflection of his lifetime of work studying the graylag geese, which live mainly in the northern countries. Lorenz's work grew out of his love for the beauty of the geese's flight which he first noticed as a boy. He believes the beauty of the natural world can encourage humans to ecological responsibility much more than penitential preaching ever can. I agree with him.

This is my last day at St. Mary's so I'm cramming. Three and a half hours in the library and a trip to the famous Notre Dame grotto where I lit candles for my particular cloud of witnesses, including Father Phil Murnion, founder of the National Pastoral Life Center in New York, who was buried eight months ago today. After the candle lighting, I lingered for a long while, soaking up clear spring air and sunshine, marveling at the tulips newly in bloom, feeling grateful to have been in South Bend for these weeks where Tom and I began our married life forty-seven years ago, and grateful to be going home to Virginia where we lived it. "Not knowing what lies before you..." Words full of personal and societal wisdom.

I'm grateful, too, for the Prayer of the Church, which has sustained me daily, and which draws my gaze to the future. I've been helped by some lines from a poem which I include these days in evening prayer.

VESPERS

... I need to pause at eventide and bring to mind

when first we saw our spinning sphere, and that,

just moments later in cosmic time, satellite photos show

wanton wounds of ravaged forests, fetid waters, sinking shores.

I need to grieve our glaciers gliding to a liquid grave:

to honor trafficked teens and bloated orphans,

Pietas sculpted by our wasting wars; I need

to deepen daunting insights: it's happening to us.[6]

As I pray these lines over and over, one evening after another, I see the communion of saints (or blessedness) extending beyond the human to all of life on earth. This is both comfort and sorrow.

An Irish Pilgrimage

One of the anthropological features of a pilgrimage is a return to the place of origins, the place of religious or tribal roots. The trip to Ireland is in the lineage of pilgrimage. Tom and I intended to visit the places of his parents' origins, on both sides of the border, and to visit for the first time a cousin of mine with whom I had been in contact for only a few years. We would be honoring our ancestors.

Pilgrimages also have the potential to engender change in the pilgrims as they pass over a threshold into the place of their beginning. An important feature of this passing over is that the pilgrims do not remain at their pilgrimage destination; they return home, changed, and their presence changes the environment of home and beyond.

Journal Entries

May 13, 2004

Today the pilgrimage begins. I go to Ireland, alone. Getting ready has been nonstop, and I have not been sleeping well. Sunday morning at Mass I was caught up in wondering if I would ever see Tom again in his old flesh, the way I used to know him. Then something in the Sunday readings got my attention; an insight, I guess. After his resurrection, people did not recognize Jesus except through his wounds. What follows is that our wounds, all kinds of hurts, including loss, will stay. They are shaping our personality, and that's how we'll recognize one another.

May 14, 2004

Thank God for a safe arrival in Dublin. The flight was cramped, longer than I remember it from the past, and noticeably short on amenities. As I maneuvered on the plane, and then in the Dublin airport with customs, luggage, finding a taxi, I realized that Tom could not have borne the stress if he had lived to undertake the trip. We had pared his life to manageable proportions. He was no longer used to the burdens of travel.

At my hotel there were two messages waiting. One that a ticket awaited me for that night's performance at the Abbey Theater of *A Midsummer Night's Dream*; the other was a phone call from my cousin Brendan to arrange a visit on Sunday. Irish hospitality was manifesting itself.

The theater surprise was that the play was in Slovenian with the text in English overhead, much as we might see in the United States for an Italian opera. The reason for this was a salute to the European Union, whose delegates were meeting in Dublin. After Act One, I bailed out, the fatigue of travel and the strain of trying to understand having caught up with me.

May 15, 2004

Today would have been Tom's seventieth birthday, the inspiration for this personal pilgrimage. I had made plans to attend an all-day debate at the Abbey Theater about "Memory and Repertoire" in the theater. The debate was really a panel which offered different and far-ranging opinions on the topic. The panelists talked about the effect of a repressive society on the theater which resulted for many years in censorship, which in turn produced periods of silence about certain topics like sexuality, women, the civil war and the great famine. Men did write about some of these topics, but did so *outside* of Ireland, like James Joyce. But always there were women, too, who wrote novels and plays in the face of censorship. They are less well known, except perhaps for Edna O'Brien.

One panelist emphasized that repertory theater, like the Abbey, has a responsibility to keep alive the classics but to refract the plays through an Irish lens. Brian Friel and Seamus Heaney are among the Irish writers who are drawn to the Greek theater, often to explore ethical issues, and then to reproduce the Greek plays in a new and fresh way. They also are responsible for bringing forth plays about Irish history like the civil war and the famine, for connecting memory to contemporary experience. And again, women are among the working Irish playwrights doing so, and this has been true since the beginning of the Abbey Theater when Lady Gregory was prominent. The debate, which probed the aesthetics and history of Irish literature, was a great way to celebrate Tom's birthday. But still, I felt the aloneness in an acute way, especially at lunchtime. This was to be expected since I didn't know anyone.

By accident, I attended a Carmelite church for evening Mass. The church was filled at 5:30 PM. Many of the congregants were shoppers on their way home from a day on Grafton Street. Afterward, I walked to the Shelburne Hotel (a long walk for me) and had an elegant dinner for this special day. The waiter, fearing my solitude, brought me two newspapers, which I happily accepted but which I didn't read. I was more interested in the passersby and the beauty of lilacs on St. Stephen's Green. I was doing what Tom liked to do, namely, observe the world.

May 16, 2004
In the morning I caught an early Sunday train to Dundalk, where my cousin Brendan lives with his wife and two adult children. A few years back he began researching our family tree and discovered that my paternal grandfather, John, and his grandfather Matthew were brothers. John emigrated to the United States while Matthew stayed on the farm. For years Brendan had worked on the border in the North as a customs official for the Republic of Ireland. There he enjoyed good relations with his British counterparts, as together they patrolled

points of entry on the border. Then, when he was transferred to Dublin, he suddenly had blocks of time during the day which he used for research in the office of public records. It was fascinating for me to learn about our common relatives and to see how one contact led him to many more. I brought him photos of my father and stories of my uncles' adventures which I had heard as a child. He drove me back to Dublin in the evening, and I realized that we had spent twelve hours together; the time seemed short. We both felt as if we had known each other all our lives. And perhaps in some mysterious way we have. Soon I go to County Mayo awaiting Celia and Jay and Myra.

May 21, 2004
We left the house in Mayo, where we stayed for almost a week, for County Cavan to search for the remaining ruins of Tom and Jay's mother's house. This has never been an easy task. The cottage is off the visible road and you have to know exactly where you're going. A guide is essential. I remembered meeting young Thomas McGovern (he's now in his late sixties) at a village funeral twenty-five years earlier. I knew he returned to the mountains of Cavan, to care for his ninety-eight-year old father, and I hoped he'd still be there. He was. Finding him took two days of dogged determination, knocking on doors, explaining our purpose, asking for help. By now, a lot of people knew we were looking for a guide. One woman who invited us for tea (which we declined and regretted later) announced her age as ninety-two. She told us that her husband died ten years earlier and that now she lives with her daughter and son-in-law. She looked wistful as she said, "It's hard without him, but we have to go on." I felt the shock of her words. Ten years and the same emptiness! Celia thanked her in Gaelic, and as we prepared to leave, the woman, in turn, blessed us in Gaelic. By now we were tired, physically and emotionally, and decided to continue our search the next day.

Crossing over the border into the British section, we found a B&B in a converted customs house staffed by John, who was young, vivacious, full of laughter and offered cut-rate prices. We took beautiful rooms across from a park with a lake. A fine dinner prepared by John (who doubles as chef) launched us into plans for the next day's search. I was to call Thomas and another Cavan man, Johnny, son of John of the Mill. The latter's line was busy but I connected with Thomas who said he would come to the customs house and lead us to the "ancestral homes." (There are actually two cottages.) He had corresponded once or twice with my Tom who noticed that Thomas had adopted more Gaelic than English in his writing. We recognized each other immediately. Amazing.

First Thomas took us to a restored house, where Tom's grandmother had been born. There were three rooms, with electricity, telephone and cable connections for television (the last time I saw the cottage it had a thatched roof and *no* electricity.) In recent years, it had been rented, although not now. Beautiful mountain views and wildflowers were everywhere. It was a very livable house but very hidden away. It is important to remember this because the romanticism of such a place can carry you into decisions (like entertaining notions of taking up residence in the remote hills of Cavan) best left alone.

The farm where Tom's mother lived is in better shape than I expected. There was no roof, but the walls were standing, as was a chimney. The dairy part of the house was recognizable as was the loft window out of which Tom's grandfather Phillip jumped to escape the constables who were after him because of his association with the Irish Republican Army. My deteriorating knee prevented me from scurrying over the ruins but we all collected stones to deliver to Tom's grave. The view from this vantage was even more striking than the former spot. And the quiet was profound.

Thomas invited us all back to his house for coffee where we learned more about him. Since he returned to the village he has been exploring the land he loves, the mountains of the north. And he'd been studying on his own, mostly archaeology, which includes hunting for artifacts. He is widely read as are so many of the Irish.

An addition to the original cottage where he was born includes a modern kitchen and a circular staircase to the upstairs. Look around the cottage and you see what is important to Thomas: a collection of CDs, a globe of the world, hand-painted tiles (his work) and a couple of peat-burning fireplaces. He is a creative, happy bachelor—a mountain man—who showed us enormous kindness, and shared what was dearest to him.

Further Reflections on Lent and Easter

My spiritual director was right all those years ago. Lent *is* a happy time, not a time of reveling, but a time of discarding clutter so you can see the beauty that is so often hidden in plain sight. The simple, the spare, the empty space and natural light have all come to the foreground to teach new ways of appreciating the commonplace.

These forty days of trying to unclutter, and the subsequent celebration of life breaking through at Eastertime have taught me simple but important lessons. One lesson, not new but worth emphasizing, is that renewed life and interdependence are entwined, and so is *known* community, with its natural bonds and familiarity, which fosters courage to embrace the unknown. We cannot live a resurrected life alone. Another lesson is that it helps to know our limitations. My short sabbatical at St. Mary's College in Notre Dame brought this lesson front and center. The sabbatical was a wonderful gift, a gift of time and space to create a piece of work, a book. It was also a gift of insight as I moved among the different generations of women: students and retired faculty, and current faculty dedicated to exploring the contributions of different cultures to contemporary Christian life. It was rich fare, but I think I came to the feast too soon after a time of inner fasting. I learned how much family and longtime friends, and the familiar rhythms of home and work are agents of renewal. An old adage says something like "timing is everything." At first I thought my timing for this sabbatical may have been off, and in some ways it was; in other ways, it wasn't.

Saint Thérèse of Lisieux says *tout est grace*—all is grace. A signal grace of the time at St. Mary's was to see more clearly the strength derived from roots, and from familiarity. Isn't that what ritual is? A connecting to the core of our lives?

The Irish pilgrimage was a ritual of connection. From the all day visit with my cousin to the discussions about memory at the Abbey Theater to the finding of the ruins of Tom's mother's cottage, the lives of familial community became more vivid. When I looked into the roofless room of the cottage that was once the dairy part of the house, I could see some family member churning the butter. The kitchen outlines are still evident. Are there children sitting around a table? In my imagination there are.

Each time I've been to the ruins I have a new appreciation for the Irish emigrants who left the beauty of the Cavan mountains for the density and dangers of American cities. That story is found all through Ireland. Why did they leave? For their children. That's the simple truth. They wanted work so they could provide for their families, and they wanted educational opportunities for their children, neither of which was available in Ireland at that time.

The same is true today. Men and women come to the borders of America, not for reasons of malice, but for reasons of hope. The question which keeps coming into my prayer is how can we welcome them? Another question is why is fear governing the discussion about immigration? A line from the poem "Vespers" comes to mind. "I need / to deepen daunting insights; it's happening to us." We are the immigrants, and if we look the other way at injustice, we are the inhospitable. And we will miss the joy of communion with these saints.

The changes engendered by these pilgrimage experiences are subtle, but real. I'm more aware of inner freedom, more willing to risk, and at the same time more appreciative of home.

FOOD FOR THOUGHT

1. In what ways might you simplify (unclutter) your life?
2. Have you ever made a "pilgrimage" to a source of roots in your own life? The house you grew up in? Your old neighborhood parish? Some place beyond the territorial borders of the United States? How did the experience affect you?
3. In the evening of life what form of creativity seems possible? Volunteer service? Trying a new art form? Strengthening a family relationship? Learning a new skill? Risking a new or renewed relationship?

RITUAL

The following two prayers are taken from *Morning and Evening Prayer of the Sisters of Mercy* for Easter Sunday.

Morning Prayer

Christ, firstborn from the dead, you triumphed over sin and set all humankind free.

Risen Savior, free us to live in newness of life as daughters of God.

Risen Savior, you came to Mary Magdalene in the quiet of the garden and revealed your presence to her:

—*Speak to our hearts, and let us know that you are with us.*

Risen Savior, you walked with the disciples on the way to Emmaus and set their hearts on fire:

—*Let our hearts burn with the desire to share the Good News.*

Risen Savior, you burst through the bonds of death to show us the power of God.

—*Give us the strength to break through attitudes that keep us from serving others.*

Risen Savior, you have a special care for the poor and the suffering:

—*Use us as instruments of your mercy for the poor and the suffering of our time.*

Risen Savior, you rise to banish alienation and bring all peoples into
unity:
—*Bring unity among all Christian churches that they may be of one heart
and one mind in you.*

Evening Prayer
Mary Magdalene was filled with wonder at your living presence. Let
us honor with grateful spirits the wonder of your risen life.
Risen Christ, you healed Mary of brokenness, fear and uncertainty:
—*Heal us and all who are broken.*
Holy One, you blessed Mary with the gift of inner quiet and peace:
—*Fill us with peace in your presence.*
Comforting Friend, you turned Mary's tears and sadness into under-
standing and confidence:
—*Grant us confident understanding of your continuing mission in this
world.*
Giver of hope, you offered Mary a sure and faithful love:
—*Make our love steadfast and enduring.*
God of all peoples and nations, you sent us Jesus to bring all into
unity:
—*Send us forth, like Mary, to tell the good news of your gospel.*[7]

CHAPTER FOUR

• PENTECOST •

A Return to the Ordinary

Coming Home

Pilgrimages are temporary. The pilgrims or seekers eventually return home, changed (as I indicated in the previous chapter), and carrying the seeds of change with them. One place I call home is my parish, Our Lady Queen of Peace Church in Arlington, Virginia. There I have experienced all kinds of change, not so much as an agent but as a subject. I've been both supported and challenged. Historically it is an African American parish staffed from its beginning in 1945 by Holy Ghost Fathers, now known as Spiritans. They are a missionary order with deep roots in Africa and Haiti. In the United States their hearts and minds and energies have been devoted to the education and welfare of people of color.

During the 1960s civil rights period, Queen of Peace was a central gathering place for those about to embark on voting rights demonstrations, for the Poor People's Campaign, and for the peace marches that filled the streets of Washington, D.C. I became acquainted with that unpretentious white stucco church when I sought advice from the pastor about how to convince my geographic parish to welcome the Catholic Interracial Council for a presentation. I was also hoping to learn something about community organizing.

It was suggested that I consult the pastor at Queen of Peace. For me, it was an unforgettable meeting. I was greeted at the door, one brisk autumn evening, by the white pastor reading aloud from Langston Hughes, an African American poet. He would read a little and then comment. His comments were along the lines of "us and you" which I finally understood was his style of identifying with the African Americans he served day in and day out. When we finally settled down in the living room and I presented my problem to him, he gave me some unexpected and disarming suggestions. Instead of helping me with community organizing—which I thought he would—he said, "You need to read the works of Evelyn Underhill." I had no idea who that might be. "She's an Anglican laywoman," he informed me, "deeply knowledgeable about the spiritual life. I think you should read and ponder what she has to say." And so began my lifelong association with Underhill's writings. What I came to realize after a while was that the pastor was telling me that if I was serious about social justice work, I had better be serious about developing depth in my spiritual life. It was some years before my husband and I became members of the church, a decision I believe was Spirit-led. The parish has been and remains noted for its welcome, true to its founders' intent.

In 1945 a small group of African American Catholics took Jesus at his word and laid the foundation for a worshipping community that would welcome all as sisters and brothers, as members of the one family of God. From that humble beginning the parish has evolved where diversity is counted as a blessing and no effort is counted too small to make a difference in ministry and service.

The parish mission statement sets forth an ideal. "Our Lady Queen of Peace Catholic Church is dedicated to witnessing the teachings of Jesus Christ, especially on the Gospel of St. Matthew, chapter 25:31–46 (which describes the criteria for judging who will enter the Kingdom of Heaven: those who feed the hungry and clothe the naked, welcome the stranger and visit prisoners). Our mission is to nurture the spirit and to encourage the potential of those we serve through liturgical celebration, education endeavors and social ministries.... As a multi-ethnic congregation, we will seek to promote racial harmony and social justice. While our primary focus is within the immediate community, we will also work to provide for the well-being of the downtrodden everywhere. In this we strive for our parish community to be a caring, sharing, and loving family." This, then, is the guiding document of the mission and ministries of Queen of Peace.

I came home from Ireland in time to celebrate Pentecost in this church that has existed explicitly under the banner of the Holy Spirit. And I was grateful to be home with my people, my extended family.

Pentecost is a time of being drenched in love, not the Hallmark variety, but the sturdy love that is of God. Evelyn Underhill writes that when we hear the words "Receive the Holy Spirit" the meaning is simply "Receive the Life of God." The emphasis is on receiving since the nature of God is to give, to pour out the love which is the divine nature. As we become more receptive to authentic love, to the Spirit, the fruits of the Spirit are felt and seen in us. Saint Paul enumerates them: love, joy, peace, long-suffering, gentleness, goodness, faithfulness, meekness, temperance—all of which have a social dimension and which can impact the environment positively. It is these fruits of the Spirit that I notice distributed within the Queen of Peace congregation.

Pentecost evening the reading for Vespers was from Isaiah (61:1–2a, 3a)

> The spirit of the Lord is upon me, because the Lord has anointed me and sent me to bring good news to the oppressed, to bind up the bro-kenhearted, to proclaim liberty to captives, and release to prisoners; to proclaim a year of the Lord's favor; to provide for those who mourn in Zion—to give them a garland instead of ashes, the oil of gladness instead of mourning, the mantle of praise instead of a faint spirit.

I read these lines with stirrings of hope that there will be energy, not only in me, but in others, too, to respond to God's call for mercy and justice. The Carmelite poet Jessica Powers offers insight into *how* to live, day by day, responsive to the Spirit.

To LIVE WITH THE SPIRIT
To live with the Spirit of God is to be a listener.
It is to keep the vigil of mystery,
earthless and still.
One leans to catch the stirring of the Spirit,
strange as the wind's will.
The soul that walks where the wind of the Spirit blows
turns like a wandering weather-vane toward love.
It may lament like Job or Jeremiah,
echo the wounded hart, the mateless dove.
It may rejoice in spaciousness of meadow
that emulates the freedom of the sky.
Always it walks in waylessness, unknowing;
it has cast down forever from its hand
the compass of the whither and the why.
To live with the Spirit of God is to be a lover.
It is becoming love, and like to Him
toward Whom we strain with metaphors of creatures:
fire-sweep and water-rush and the wind's whim.
The soul is all activity, all silence;
and though it surges Godward to its goal,
it holds, as moving earth holds sleeping noonday,
the peace that is the listening of the soul. [1]

The poem is like a map, helpful as I try to chart my course through Ordinary Time alive in the Holy Spirit, noting the fruits of Spirit as they appear often unexpectedly. One has to lean—not be rigid—to catch the stirring. This is important to remember.

Journal Entries

My journal is thinning out. There are fewer and fewer entries. Am I experiencing ennui? Confusion? Or am I at last listening more than talking? Is my soul listening?

The rituals of this past year have been meaningful markers as I journeyed inward to try to locate my new center. And now the rituals of the first year are coming to the end.

June 28, 2004

One of the most touching final moments in Ireland was when our family friend Austin, who lives in Mayo, went into the fields and picked a bunch of heather for me which he trimmed and tied and presented as a memento of County Mayo. I brought it home to dry and to remember how beautiful the simple things of Ireland are.

Looking back on the past week I realize how hard the week before the first anniversary of Tom's death has been. I relived the details of his last week on earth: what he ate, what he drank, our time at the Tides Inn where we had gone for a mini-vacation, the last meal I cooked for him—and his cough. The cough was diagnosed as acute bronchitis, with doctors telling me his lungs were clear. No one mentioned it might be congestive heart failure. The truth is he coughed himself to death.

The family Mass for this first anniversary was celebrated at the church down the street from our home, not at Queen of Peace which does not have a Mass every day. The Irish priest who chairs the Friends of All Hallows was the celebrant and many friends from different generations were present—a bulwark against too much sorrow.

After Mass I went to my office—a wise decision. By evening I was calm enough to host a dinner for family and close friends at the restaurant where we held the post-funeral dinner last year. Also at the restaurant were large groups of injured Iraq War veterans who arrived in buses from Walter Reed hospital in Washington. The result was overworked and overwrought waiters. It took a long, long time to be served. But as one of our party commented, "For the vets we can put up with a lot." The most moving part of the vets' presence was to see these young wounded trying to walk about helped by their wives, or fiancés or friends—a picture of changed life in the United States in the wake of war. Queen of Peace, pray for us.

July 10, 2004

I am still digesting the stimulating and hopeful ideas put forth at a conference I attended in Philadelphia a few days ago. It was sponsored by a group representing Yale Divinity School, *America* magazine, Boston College and a number of Catholic foundations. It was a beautifully crafted working conference on "The American Catholic Church Leadership Roundtable 2004." Governance in the church was a major focus.

The Wharton Business School was the conference site and first-class technology was at our disposal: videos and films, voting machines and PowerPoint. What I found especially striking was the lack of anger. There was no projecting onto the church all the problems of the world, personal or corporate. The planners and organizers clearly love the church, and in this era of church scandals, want only to help the church's leaders move forward with integrity. Many of these gifted laity—leaders in various secular fields—were eager to share "best practices" with the bishops and other leaders. This can be an enormous plus for the church which is, in truth, reeling from the sex abuse scandals.[2]

One of the graced sidebars of the conference was finding out about the children's May pilgrimages to Lourdes. There are scholarships for a disabled or sick child (and the accompanying parent) who need financial assistance. The doctor who told me about the pilgrimage thought that Mary Kate's son, who has neurological damage, would qualify. The question now is whether Mary Kate will be open to this possibility. We'll see.

Another grace was discovering that a conference attendee, some-one I've known for years, now retired from his philanthropic work, is painting portraits in his retirement. With the passing of the first anniversary of Tom's death, and the year of rituals over, the future opens up so wide and empty. How to live in the emptiness is the ques-tion constantly before me, although lately I've had the idea that a por-trait of Tom in the entryway might help. I was beginning to research how that might come to pass. A conversation with the philanthropist turned portrait painter revealed that he does his work from photo-graphs, and he's open to trying this new project.

So many blessings in the city of brotherly-sisterly love.

July 16, 2004
Mary Kate has been in Arlington with Conor for evaluations and continuing medical therapies. I told her about the Lourdes possibility and she is not only open to the idea but enthusiastic. She said, "We're working hard with Conor, but we would be grateful for a miracle." Now she and I must get the wheels turning. She'll need a statement from the doctors who care for Conor, and I must arrange for the other necessary paper work.

July 22, 2004
Today is the feast of Saint Mary Magdalene, patron of my home parish where I grew up in Queens, New York. In the garden of the church was a statue of the saint clinging to the cross. In later years, I thought it was reminiscent of Bernini's "St. Teresa in Ecstasy."

I did my stint at St. George's Pantry today. This monthly volun-teer service is always in memory of Tom, who was closer to the poor and the homeless than I will ever be. When I'm there goodness and faithfulness (fruits of the Holy Spirit) are in the forefront of con-sciousness. Underhill says of these that we are inclined to think of them as the supreme virtues of the plain man. In another place she says, "Faithfulness is consecration in overalls. It is the steady acceptance and performance of the common duty and immediate task without any reference to personal preference—because it is there to be done and so is a manifestation of the Will of God."[3] That was the way Tom entered into all manner of work: his professional work and his ongoing commitment to the poor. And it's what I see at the pantry. People work hard stocking shelves, supervising the clients and keeping records because they are faithful.

August 10, 2004

This evening I searched again for the book *From Nineveh to New York.* I have been looking for it all summer wanting to read more deeply about the strange and dangerous place called Iraq. The book is based on an exhibit with the same name which Tom and I had seen five or six years ago in New York City. I couldn't find it in July and I couldn't find it tonight. I went through every bookcase: in the dining room, in my work room, in the guest room, which houses Tom's special collection. Nothing. I broke down in tears and an awful feeling of being deprived of Tom and his guidance, which had been so prominent in the early months after his death, welled up in me. I realize that recently a terrible inner barrenness had been growing in me along with doubts that I would ever see him again. What was the church trying to get us all to believe? Suppose we *never* see our beloved dead again? Perhaps we have to be at some point of personal and particular development—enlightenment, realization, whatever. Is that it? All I saw this night was nothing, nothing. In my agitated state, love seemed so cruel, so tricky. I wailed as I did in the weeks after his death. I challenged Tom, and God, about the book. This was to be the sign that God had not taken Tom away from me, away from this last home we shared. I could see the cover of the book in my mind, a kind of orange softcover book. I would give them—Tom and God—one more chance. Where was it? It occurred to me that Tom might have loaned it to someone, not an unthinkable possibility. After a glass of wine and a rather tasteless dinner, fear and a dull resignation grew larger. Tom is no longer here to help. I am really on my own, I told myself. I sat in a chair near the dining room bookcase, turned to look at a filled shelf, and picked up a hardcover *green* book. *From Nineveh to New York.* It was (is)—I believe—a sign, a sacramental. Of course it was always there. In some sense everything is always there, always *here*. Nothing is lacking, says the wisdom of the Tao.

> Be content with what you have;
> Rejoice in the way things are.
> When you realize there is nothing lacking
> the whole world belongs to you.[4]

The problem is that blindness and willfulness (both of which I displayed in great measure this evening) cloud reality. More tears, this time in gratitude, confident that Tom would remain with me. I took the book to bed tonight.

August 19, 2004

Once again I offer a small portion of time, two and a half hours, at the pantry, keeping track of how many desolate and desperate people come for a small supply of vegetables, protein, fruits, drinks and a few, very few, sweets. The brief conversations with them are coming more easily. Our clients bring to mind two other fruits of the Spirit: meekness and temperance, which Underhill terms humility and moderation. God's love is manifested not in some peculiar supernatural manner but in ordinary human nature. In God's family circle, she says, there is room for the childish and the imperfect and the naughty, but the uppish is always out of place. The men and women who frequent the pantry come just as they are, no pretense (although occasionally there is someone with delusions). Often they are victims of intemperance regarding alcohol or drugs or other things. Most of them, however, are genuinely grateful for a can of beets and some fruit juice. Although I felt tired during my time there, I was also consoled at the thought of the book—the sacramental—waiting for me at home.

September 2, 2004

A day of preparation for a trip to Rhode Island to visit friends and then on to Eastern Point near Gloucester Massachusetts for an eight-day silent retreat. Even though finding *From Nineveh to New York* strengthened my belief in the power of love, I am still haunted by the question: What if this present life is all there is? Will I never see Tom again? Then this thought rises up that we will see each other but in a different way. Perhaps it is in the communion of saints, in the enfolding of all in God. But recognition? How? We learn to recognize one another through prayer is the gentle answer, through coming close to the heart of God who is love and who abides in love. Actually Tom communicates this to me each day, but I'm fighting so hard. Fighting fear. I fear the trip, whether it will be too hard physically or emotionally. I also fear the retreat which is a huge unknown.

Retreat at Eastern Point, September 7–15, 2007

Beginning

The retreat opens with a gathering of those who will be seeking God during the coming week. We introduce ourselves to the group and focus on the grace we seek. After this evening's plenary session we will be in solitude and prayer, speaking only to the spiritual director assigned to us for the week. There is expectancy in the air. And hope.

The Jesuit director of the retreat house reads a passage from Isaiah 55 about how the Lord will satisfy us. Questions are posed: What really does satisfy? What truly gives delight? God's word is potently present. "Come to me, listen, live."

It is time to articulate what grace I seek from these days apart. The words are formulated in my heart. I ask to have some idea of how God wants me to spend whatever future is left to me. I ask for courage and peace in following God's will for me. I ask for courage and peace for those for whom I will be praying during this privileged time, and who will be with me in prayer:

My children and their children
The children of the world, especially those ravaged by war
The Woodstock community which has a major commitment to understanding all sides of the globalization issue
Friends who bear in their bodies terrible illnesses

The night before I arrived at Eastern Point I had two dreams which may be introductory to the retreat:

First dream. I planted a tree which looked like a stick. It needed care, and I looked around for someone to water it and generally cultivate it. I found a man and asked him to help me but he hesitated saying the tree was not from his nursery. I assured him it was and then walked to the back of the house where there was a blooming garden, laden with vegetables and flowers, some of which were staked. It was obviously well cared for, but nearby was a cabin with sand all over the porch and the steps. I set about clearing away the sand.

Second dream. I was in the basement of a dark house. My daughter Celia called to me through a basement window, telling me to leave immediately. She said a dangerous person was in the house. I questioned her but she kept insisting that I leave. I thought I could lock the door against the danger but she insisted that wouldn't work. Finally I left and locked the door after me. The house was drenched in darkness.

I wonder what insight these dreams may have.

September 8, 2004
Today the church celebrates the birth of Mary of Nazareth. It is also my son Colum's baptismal day, and it is raining. The rain is a gift from Hurricane Frances, and the Isaiah reading seems so apt with God giving seed to the sower and bread to the eater. It's apt for baptism too, rain strong and sure as God's Word.

I brought with me two books, one by Mary Oliver (a book of poems), the other Edith Hamilton's *The Greek Way*. These are my only companions on this retreat, besides the Scripture that my wise and experienced director assigns.

In Oliver's "Morning Poem" she asks the reader if you have ever dared to be happy or to pray. Clearly she means really pray. I turn over the question about happiness in my mind and in my heart. I have been meditating on Jeremiah 29:11–14, the Scripture assigned by my director. God speaks to Jeremiah: "Surely I know the plans I have for you, for your welfare, not your harm, to give you a future with hope."

I ask, "What are those plans, Lord?" and the answer is "You will find me (and the plans?) if you seek me with all your heart." That's the key: *with all your heart*. It's time to get beyond half-heartedness. I go on with Jeremiah and the Lord is assuring: I will lead you back. I understand that to mean *home*. I love the word *home*. Often when I feel stressed I say to myself, perhaps to God, "I want to go home." I remember my dream about the dark house. Even with darkness and danger I did not want to leave. It was home.

I think, too, of the other dream: the tree, the garden, sand on the steps. I'm starting here, on retreat, to sweep away the accumulation. The garden is growing without my direct action, but I need to be responsible for clearing the sand. I know that Someone is providing for me. I know that God is close to the broken-hearted. Could God's plan be simply to live life fully, abundantly?

September 9, 2004

This morning after breakfast, watching the ocean and a myriad of birds, I was drawn to pick up the bird guide and read a bit. How little I know about the natural world, how much I want to know about God's magnificent creation. I want to be able to recognize a purple finch or a barn swallow. Mary Oliver writes about slowing down for happiness. Watching birds, studying them, requires a slowing down.

BIRDS

Are they aware of the air?

Are we aware of the infinite ocean

of love and light that sustain us in being?

Whether or not the birds are in the know

they take flight,

confident and assured in their native land.

We, though gifted with consciousness,

remained grounded,

blind to the life that would life us to flight.

I envy the wren and the gull,

their freedom from unending introspection.[5]

Actually, at this moment, my task is introspection.

I read in my other companion, *The Greek Way* Plato's advice to know thyself and to do nothing in excess. Back to my dream about the sand. What does it signify? I think it points to the habits of home which are filled with the stimulation of friends, family and work, exactly what I needed so badly during my time at St. Mary's. But here, on retreat, the stimulation is all interior.

Last evening in the library I read the *Boston Globe*, and even that brief perusal put me in a different place, psychologically and spiritually (newspapers can be overstimulating). I must sweep, morning and evening.

New Scriptures are assigned. Isaiah 43:1–7; 45:4–6; 46:3–4. The pouring out of unconditional love is overpowering, so much so that only tears will do. In Isaiah 46 I read, "Even to your old age I am he / Even when you turn gray I will carry you." Side by side with the Mary Oliver poem "The Wild Geese" which has a line about not having to be good, the vastness and depth of God's love is almost too much. My director asks about the power of "home" in my life. "What does it mean?" she asks. I answer, "Tom was home for me; and safety and security conjure up home." But in truth, in the last two years of Tom's life I was providing security for him, or so I thought! But now it is clear that it is God who provides.

The homily at Mass today was about loving our enemies. The homilist noted that God has no enemies.

This afternoon I went into high gear, not meditating or really praying but creating an action plan for myself. Avoidance of prayer, perhaps? Or maybe simply being true to what I am: an activist.

By evening I was exhausted and went to sleep early, and then awoke at 3:30 AM. I had been dreaming that I was standing in a lobby when a man appeared and handed me a copy of a book for which I had written a chapter. I noticed the title of the book had been changed from a sociological title to simply *Saving Grace*. I asked why the change and the man said when he studied the content the new title came to him. I knew that included my chapter; I felt joy that I had a contribution to make, a small piece of saving grace. The effect on me in the middle of the night was a deep awareness of all the people who have enriched my life, from the beginning to this very moment. If I have contributed anything of saving grace, it is because of them, of what they have given not only to me but to the world. This morning's homily fit: The measure you give is the measure that will be given to you.

September 10, 2004
At lunchtime I sat in the back of the dining room so I had a view not only of the ocean but of my fellow retreatants. After only a few days in silence and minimal interactions (just enough to clean up after meals) I can see something of their unique personalities, and I can also see how the Isaiah 43 passage fits them. They are precious to God. So many are aged, and more than a few infirm in one way or another. We are all limping like wrestlers with God. But their beauty is becoming more visible, shining through the surface.

After lunch I went outside to observe more closely the beauty of water and rock and bird. I even tried to navigate a path to a rock formation, setting aside my inherent resistance to such adventures. If it weren't for Tom I would never have done so many wonderful things: the hike down Mt. Washington in 1966 with four small children; climbing from a boat onto one of the Farne Islands off the coast of Northumbria, where birds of the North Atlantic nest; the lenten walk through the Judean desert to Jericho. Tom gave me courage. But I must not forget that God is our ultimate provider.

Mass was a work of art. The priest, who is Slavic, used prelude music from Rachmaninoff and Rimsky-Korsakov. The homily (given before the readings) was superb. He began with the Olympics (a nice fit for my Greek reading) and contrasted the "real" Olympics with its goal of someone winning, being the best, and the "Special Olympics" where everyone wins. In his opinion Saint Paul's race analogy fit the latter. Those spoken words were an extension of my lunchtime experience, and provided clarity for me that "saving grace"—my dream image—is really about the community. We are saved in community.

September 11, 2004
A beautiful day much like the day of the tragedy three years ago. Again, the dining room was the setting this morning for some insight. I realized I was less lonely with this group of people, largely unknown to me, than I often am with my old and dear friends. Sometimes, the socializing is a distraction, something a woman friend, recently widowed, believes is necessary. Distraction, she says, keeps her from despair. But here, on retreat, there are no distractions. Everything is of a piece.

This evening I again read the *Boston Globe*, and that was a moment of grace. I read about an organization of women who lost their spouses in the September 11 attacks. They came together to go beyond their personal experience of widowhood to form a nonprofit group, "Beyond the 11th" to aid widows affected by war and terrorism. They realized that though they sorrowed, they were not left destitute as so many women in wartime are. The organization they created is partnering with some other organizations and has become a significant presence in Afghanistan. Their goals are simple: to provide financial assistance for present survival needs and training for future self-sufficiency; and, on a personal level, to foster connections between American and Afghan women.

The story opens up endless possibilities for women to reach beyond the borders of individualism, to communion with women whose needs are great.

Still pondering the possibilities of connecting with this new organization I went outside where I and others witnessed a most beautiful sunset. For a long time we stood together, happy in the presence of such intense beauty. Reading the article about the Afghan widows also made me feel more intensely alive.

The silence of the retreat enables us to be much more aware of everything around us and within us; there are so many different ways to experience life, and renewal of life, resurrection.

The homilist today, a blind woman, said the important thing is what we do with the circumstances of our lives. She is a witness to that.

September 12, 2004
In the early morning lying in bed, thinking of Tom, and aware of the healing underway I said to him, "We'll keep your memory alive, the children and I, and our friends, and the homeless you worked with so joyfully." Then I looked at the crucifix and I asked, "Who's keeping your memory alive? How is it happening?" I went to the Bible and it fell open to Mark 14, the story of the woman with the jar of ointment, who anointed the feet of Jesus. Such loving extravagance. Jesus said that woman would be remembered, but the truth is Jesus and the unknown woman are forever linked. Without him there would be no remembrance.

I've been thinking hard about relationships. Aren't blessings a means of connecting? Is it not true that the measure you give is the measure you receive? It's all of a piece. God is weaving our lives, and while we sometimes undo the weaving, or mess up the design, the weaving goes on.

The Retreat Ends

The retreat has led to a place of deeper belief and trust in the saving grace of God, from dreams that occurred before and during the retreat, to a gifted spiritual director tuned to human experience, to Scripture that seemed crafted for the day. Poetry enhanced it all. Tears watered the inner garden. Awareness of the beauty and struggle of those around me, the reverent artistic liturgies—all these have been part of God's weaving.

A major breakthrough was recognizing that I've been clinging to the image of my "broken heart" much like a badge of honor. It's time to let it go. This does not mean giving up the remembrance of Tom; the living must keep memory alive. But right now I feel that *I* am very much alive. God told me so in different ways, and I know it deep within. I'm tasting happiness.

The experience of community has been revelation. It is not the community of people I know who love and support me. Rather, in the company of strangers immersed in this silence I grew in knowledge of them in all their uniqueness. I saw the marks of Christ which they bear. William Wordsworth wrote in *Tintern Abbey* that we see into the life of things. Of course. In this atmosphere you can see more clearly the richness of life, variegated. We are a bit like Chaucer's pilgrims, on our way, everyone carrying some burden. This kind of community is truly a reflection of the communion of saints. The retreat is a snapshot of people, strangers, all intimately longing for God in the company of one another. This may be the way we shall live in the next stage of the risen life; a whole stream of human life and love together in God.

There's been a turn on this pilgrimage path. Since Tom's death I've prayed mostly to him; the retreat has brought me back into conversation with God. It's also brought me to some understanding of Jesus' words about there being no marriage in heaven. I think I see now what he meant. Marriage is a special form of communion for this life; the resurrected life is lived in communion with many. It's the overflowing love of God that becomes ever more inclusive until finally, we are all in all.

Elizabeth LeSeur, a little-known mystic, believed that relational community is not interrupted by death, but continues in death. Our challenge is to be related to different others, to experience ourselves as together the Body of Christ. All of this is about wholeness, of the deep connection between the resurrection of whole persons and the communion of saints.

I go home more whole than when I came, more alive in body and soul, anticipating the joy of ordinary days and nights, open to the future God hopes for me. I can feel the Breath of Life.

FOOD FOR THOUGHT

1. Have you ever been drawn to go on pilgrimage to a sacred site? A saint's shrine? The Holy Land? If you have done so, remember how it was for you. If not, what would help you to go?
2. Who are the people to whom you feel deeply connected? Do they help you to move through the losses of everyday life?
3. Have you ever made a silent retreat? How did that experience infuse your everyday life? How might you arrange for quiet times in your daily life?

RITUAL

• William Wordsworth wrote:

> With an eye made quiet
> By the power of harmony
> And the deep power of joy,
> We see into the life of things.[6]

Give thanks and praise to God for the life you now see.

All through the year after Tom's death I had prayed to understand what I truly desired. After the retreat I knew: It was simply to be open to whatever the future holds. The result has been a sense of anticipation and calm. Still there are days when I feel consumed with longing. I miss the intimacy of marriage in its many dimensions: conversations, silence, the pleasure of closeness, the sharing of space, intellectual stimulation, the daily rituals of dinner and bedtime and awakening.

On the other hand the ongoing communication with Tom continues, and guidance is always available. In this different way of relating we are no longer struggling with each other as we did from time to time during our marriage. While we shared a common ground of values and interests, we had our differences. But with the passage of years and the gift of memory, we came to know that we would get through the rough patches. We also realized that intimacy tends to be cyclical: a coming together and a moving apart. Once that was learned the cycle seemed friendly. And with the finality of death the difficulties tend to fade.

What remains strong is how necessary it is to give and receive love, with all the uncertainties and struggles, and how many faces of love there are. In our efforts to be human God does not leave us to fend for ourselves. To be open to newness—to resurrection—is the ongoing challenge we all face. In community—communion—we are reminded that everything is possible. Evening comes and morning follows; as it was in the beginning is now and will be forever.

NOTES

FRONTISPIECE

1. Andrew Marvell, "To His Coy Mistress" in *Top 500 Poems*, ed. William Harmon (New York: Columbia University Press, 1992).

PREFACE

1. The account of my husband's death was first published as an article "Broken Heart—Sacred Heart" in *Radical GRACE*, a publication of the Center for Action and Contemplation (Volume 19, No. 1, January—March 2006). Used with permission.

2. See Robert Kinast, *What Are They Saying About Theological Reflection?* (Mahwah, N.J.: Paulist, 2000).

3. Joan Chittister, O.S.B., in *Just War, Lasting Peace: What Christian Traditions Can Teach Us*. Dolores Leckey, ed. (Orbis, 2006), p. 34.

4. Regina Bechtle, S.C., in *National Catholic Reporter*, June 17, 2005.

CHAPTER TWO

1. Anne Porter, *Living Things (Collected Poetry)*. (Hanover, N.H.: Steerforth, 2006), p. 12. Anne Porter, now in her nineties, is the widow of painter Fairfield Porter. They raised five children together. She wrote poetry throughout her lifetime but she did not seek to publish her work until long after her husband's death. Her first collection, *An Altogether Different Language* was a 1994 National Book Award Finalist.

2. Robert F. Morneau, unpublished poem.

3. Washington Irving, *The Sketchbook* (London: Collins), pp. 218-219.

4. Alain, in *Alain on Happiness*, "The Cult of the Dead" (Evanston, Ill.: Northwestern University Press, 1989), p. 165.

5. Frederick E. Crowe, S.J., "Complacency and Concern in the Risen Life," a paper presented at the Lonergan Workshop, June 13, 1997.

CHAPTER THREE

1. George Herbert, Love (III), in Robert Morneau, *"Ashes to Easter,"* Lenten *Meditations* (New York: Crossroad, 1996).

2. Morneau, *Lenten Meditations.*

3. Quoted in John O'Donahue, *Divine Beauty: The Invisible Embrace* (London: Bantam, 2003).
4. George Herbert, lines from different versions of "Easter" in *The Temple* (New York: Paulist)
5. See Gail Porter Mandell, *One Woman's Life*, 1994 Madeleva Lecture (New York: Paulist, 1994).
6. Terri Mackenzie, S.H.C.J., "Vespers", unpublished poem.
7. (It is possible to substitute the first person singular in the responses, especially since many readers may be praying alone. However, as awareness of our connection to and insertion in the communion of saints grows, the plural will seem appropriate.)

CHAPTER FOUR

1. Jessica Powers, "To Live with the Spirit," in *Selected Poetry of Jessica Powers.* Robert Morneau and Regina Siegfried, eds. (Washington, D.C.: 1999) All copyrights, Carmelite Monastery, Pewaukee, WI. Used with permission.
2. See the Web page for The National Leadership Roundtable on Church Management, www.nlrcm.org.
3. Evelyn Underhill, *Fruits of the Spirit* (London: Longmans, Green & Co., 1956), p. 27.
4. *Tao Te Ching,* by Stephen Mitchell (New York: Harper Perennial, 1991).
5. Robert F. Morneau, "Birds," unpublished poem.
6. William Wordsworth, *Tintern Abbey,* in *The Top 500 Poems.*

Books

Buechner, Frederick. *Listen to Your Life: Daily Meditations* with George Connor (San Francisco: Harper, 1992).

Giving Sorrow Words: Poems of Strength and Solace (Washington, D.C.: National Association for Poetry Therapy Foundation).

Greene, Dana. *Evelyn Underhill: Artist of the Infinite Life* (New York: Crossroad, 1990).

James, P.D. *Time To Be in Earnest* (New York: Random House, 2001).

Johnson, Elizabeth. *Truly Our Sister: A Theology of Mary in the Communion of Saints* (New York: Continuum, 2003).

Kelsey, Morton. *Dreams, A Way To Listen to* God (New York: Paulist, 1979)

Kenyon, Jane. *Otherwise: New and Selected Poems* (St. Paul: Graywolf, 1996).

Korad Lorenz, *The Year of the Greylag Goose.* Robert Martin, trans. (New York: Harcourt Brace Jovanovich, 1978).

Leckey, Dolores. *Winter Music: A Life of Jessica Powers* (Maryland: Rowan and Littlefield, 1992).

Morrison, Mary C. *Let Evening Come: Reflections on Aging* (New York: Doubleday, 1998).

Underhill, Evelyn. *Fruits of the Spirit, Light of Christ, Abba* (London: Longmans, Green & Co., 1956).

Other Media

"Contemporary Canticles of Earth" in the Super Video-CD *Wake to Wonderment,* available from Ministry of the Arts, 800-354-3504; www.ministryofthearts.org.

Madaleva Lectures, a series on women's spirituality, sponsored by St. Mary's College, Notre Dame, and published annually by Paulist Press.

"Speaking of Faith" is an NPR program broadcast in many cities. Readers may read about the many themes addressed thorough an internet newsletter available at www.speakingoffaith.org. Subjects as varied as women in the world of Islam to God and natural disasters are discussed weekly.

Weavings is an elegant journal which promotes spiritual growth and leadership by exploring how God's life and human lives are being woven together in the world. Published bimonthly by Upper Room Ministries, Nashville, TN.

INDEX

Abbey Theater, 47, 58, 63
Abraham, 51
Adam, 54
Advent, 26
Alain, 36–37, 39
Alain on Happiness, 36–37
"Alice's Restaurant," 20
All Hallows, 15–16
All Hallows College (Dublin), 46–47
America magazine, 72
Andrew and Paul of Korea, Saints, 25
Angelus, 49
Annunciation, 12, 20, 49–50
Arlington Partnership for Affordable
  Housing (APAH), 6
Ash Wednesday, 10
Ashes to Easter, 43–44

Bad Boll, Germany, 4
Bennett, John, 8
bereavement workshop, 13–14
Book of Morning and Evening Prayer, 23,
  25, 64
Boston College, 72
"The Breaking of the Bread," 2, 3
Butler's Lives of the Saints, 11

Campbell, Jim, O.P., 38
Carmelite spirituality, 30
catacombs of Priscilla, 2
Catholic Interracial Council, 67
"Catholic Traditions of Peace and War,"
  16
Catholic University of America
  (Washington, D.C.), 7
Cayetano, Saint, 25
Cecilia, Saint, 10
Chittister, Joan, 16
Christiansen, Drew, S.J., 41
Cletus, Pope, 10
Cloisters (New York), 20–21
coinherence, 37
Columbia Gardens, 1–2
communion of saints, xvii–xviii, 34–35
"Complacency and Concern in the Risen
  Life," 39–40

Compline, xix
conversion, defined, xv
Crowe, Frederick, S.J., 39–40
Cumberland Gap, 48
Curry, Katie, 14–15

Dahlgren Chapel (Georgetown
  University), 44–45
dead, talking to, xix. *See also* communion
  of saints
Decree on the Laity, 50
Decree on Poverty, 18
The Diary of Anne Frank, 9
Die Walküre (Richard Wagner), 17
Dionysius the Aeropagite, 11
Dolphin, Kathleen, 51
Domingo, Placido, 17
Dublin, Ireland, 58
Dundalk, Ireland, 58

Easter, 1, 62
"Easter" (Herbert), 53
Economic Justice for All, 6
Epiphany, 35–36
Evening Prayer, xix

Felicity, Saint, 10
"The First Mountain of Thomas
  Merton," 14
Friel, Brian, 59
Freiderklinic, 4
From Nineveh to New York, 74–75, 76

Georgetown University. *See* Dahlgren
  Chapel; Woodstock Theological
  Center
Grail community (Loveland, Ohio), 23
The Greek Way (Hamilton), 78, 79
Greene, Dana, 8

Hampl, Patricia, 8
Heaney, Seamus, 59
Herbert, George, 43–44, 53
Hinsdale, Mary Ann, I.H.M., 55
Holy Cross Abbey, 44–45
Hughes, Langston, 68